ALL
BETTER
NOW

ALL
BETTER
NOW

A memoir by

EMILY WING SMITH

DUTTON BOOKS

DUTTON BOOKS

AN IMPRINT OF PENGUIN RANDOM HOUSE LLC

375 Hudson Street, New York, NY 10014

Names: Smith, Emily Wing, 1980- author.
Title: All better now: a novel / by Emily Wing Smith.
Description: New York, NY: Dutton Books, [2016] | Audience: 12 up.?
Identifiers: LCCN 2015020679 | ISBN 9780525426240 (hardback)
Subjects: LCSH: Smith, Emily Wing, 1980—Mental health. | Depression,
Mental—Juvenile literature. | Depressed persons—Biography. | Depression,
Mental—Biography. | Children with disabilities—Development. | Brain—Tumors—
Juvenile literature. | Tumors in children—Juvenile literature. | BISAC: JUVENILE
NONFICTION / Biography & Autobiography / General. | JUVENILE NONFICTION
/ Health & Daily Living / Physical Impairments. | JUVENILE NONFICTION / Social
Issues / Depression & Mental Illness.
Classification: LCC RC537.S65 2016 | DDC 616.85/270092—dc23
LC record available at http://lccn.loc.gov/2015020679

Printed in the United States of America

1 3 5 7 9 10 8 6 4 2

DESIGN BY IRENE VANDERVOORT
EDITED BY JULIE STRAUSS-GABEL

Text set in Palatino

For Holden:
Birthday buddy, book buddy, best buddy

AUTHOR'S NOTE:

The truth can be embarrassing. Those who know me know that my truth is *always* embarrassing. In wishing to avoid potential embarrassment to those for whom embarrassment is not an hourly occurrence, names and identifying characteristics of certain people have been changed.

Meanwhile, I signed on for this. So let my messy, embarrassing truth begin.

PROLOGUE:

HOW I'M LIVING STILL

I ask myself: *How am I living still?*

And how I ask it depends on the day.

Most mornings I wake up Woo-Head. A brief etymology: woozy-head became *Wooze-Head* became *Woo-Head*. Woo-Head is this headache hybrid that isn't made up of different kinds of pain, exactly. It's dizziness and it's light-headedness, and it's a tremble that starts between my temples and comes out the right side of my body. Bad Hand gets the shakes.

Usually I can stand up. I put on my glasses. I stagger to the bathroom mirror and stare into my eyes. Sometimes my pupils are big still and the same size, and I know that Woo-Head will dissipate, so I get ready for the day.

But sometimes my pupils are already constricted even though there's no light, and my head is spinning so fast, and I fall to the floor. And those are the mornings I ask myself: *How am I living still?* I take my emergency meds that only halfway help and go back to bed, and this will be a long day, one with no writing and no reading and—*How am I living still?*

Every once in a great while, though, I wake up and there's no Woo-Head, and I get out of bed to make sure it's not a trick. I wash my hair and I tilt my head back and still—no Woo-Head. I think, *After everything that's happened, here I am, washing my hair.* There's no Woo-Head, there's no pain, and Bad Hand even helps out, rubbing shampoo into my scalp. My fingers gloss over the incision on the back of my head and the scars on the top of my head and nope, no pain, none at all, and I think: *How am I living still?*

How am I living my dream, being a writer, publishing books and hanging out with writer friends? How am I living with a man who adores me, who never gets fed up with Woo-Head or Bad Hand or demands a normal wife whose pupils are always the same size?

How am I living still? I ask God, but it's not really a question, because I know Him well enough to know He won't answer me. Not yet.

How am I living still? I say, and I know He knows that what I mean is: *Thank you.*

The Children's Center graduation ensemble, complete with hat.

THE FIRST GRADUATION DAY

It is Graduation Day at The Children's Center.

I am the only one graduating, but we all wear hats—construction-paper hats we've decorated ourselves. I made a green one with a rainbow stretching across it because I love to draw rainbows at The Children's Center, with a box of crayons that isn't missing any colors. The stickers underneath it are in a pattern, because even more than I love to draw rainbows, I love patterns. I am seven years old.

Usually I come to The Children's Center with just my mom, but today is Graduation Day, so Juliana is there, too. Juliana chose a pink crown and put lots of red stickers on it, and she looked happy. But now Juliana isn't happy. A big sister can tell. And I can tell that Juliana is wondering: *Who is this lady? Why is her arm around me?*

The lady is Marsha. Marsha used to live in Egypt and

once gave me an Egyptian calendar. I pretended I could speak Egyptian for a long time after that, and I would show my calendar to the other kids who lived in Driftwood Park Apartments and speak Egyptian to them.

I'm not like the other kids in Driftwood Park.

Marsha is my friend at The Children's Center. We play together every week. She has boxes full of art supplies and lets me choose what I want to do. Sometimes we make masks, or paint watercolor landscapes, or try papier-mâché. Whatever I want. One day Marsha said gently, "Why don't we finish one of the projects we've started?" and she showed me the portfolio of half-finished artwork. It made my heart hurt to see them there, forgotten, and I started to cry.

Other times we do puzzles. They are the kind of puzzles that trick you because each question is harder than the last one. I can usually get just as far as we have time for, so I fill up all the time answering, answering, answering. One day Marsha showed me pictures. Each picture was missing something, and I had to tell her what it was. They were easy, like a bicycle missing a wheel or a comb missing one of its teeth. I love that the plastic comb bristles are called teeth, and I love that Marsha looked impressed when I called them teeth. Adults are my favorite people to impress, even though I'm not supposed to call Marsha an adult. At The Children's Center, you must call adults "big people," and I try very hard to remember this rule, even though I think it sounds stupid.

Marsha showed me a picture of a teacup. It was a perfect white teacup on a fragile saucer. I imagined a Japanese woman sipping from a teacup like this: sleek black hair done up in chopsticks, face pale and with only a hint of a smile, and nimble fingers curled around the cup's base. I was so busy imagining that I didn't remember to answer. When Marsha prompted me, I said: "A design." *This teacup should have a rose design*, I thought. *A delicate pink rose would be perfect.*

I could tell by the small crumpling of Marsha's face that this wasn't the right answer. *Think*, her face said. *Think again.* But I couldn't think. I had no idea what this cup—this perfect teacup—was missing. I cried little cries, at first, but little cries always turn into big cries with me. Marsha said that it was okay; we didn't have to keep going. I wanted to keep going, *had* to keep going, but I couldn't say that through the big cries.

Marsha let me be alone. I could hear her in the hall, talking to my mother, but I couldn't hear what they were saying. Probably that I was a failure. I felt like one. I'd always felt like one. I would probably not get to graduate.

I do get to graduate. And I know why: They don't want me around anymore. I don't blame them. Even *I* don't want myself around anymore. I have to be around myself, but they don't. Marsha tells me no, that's not why. She promises. But it's funny, how little I believe her.

Even though it makes me sad, it does not make my heart hurt—it is not a big enough sadness to cry about. I will miss Marsha, but now that I won't see Marsha, maybe my mom won't see Dr. John, who she talks to while I do puzzles and art projects. Maybe now that I am graduating, Mom won't be sad anymore—a heart-hurting, big-enough-to-cry-about sad.

It is Graduation Day at The Children's Center.

Maybe I am all better now.

THE CHILDREN'S CENTER

PSYCHOLOGICAL EVALUATION

Emily Wing
Age: 6 years, 0 months
Examiner: Marsha R. Blanche, PhD
Licensed Psychologist

REASON FOR REFFERAL:
   Aggressive, hostile, power struggles with mother

BACKGROUND INFORMATION:
   Emily is the oldest child of Robert and Diana Wing.
   She has a younger sister, Juliana, and a baby brother.
   Father is an attorney; mother stays home with the
   children.

   Relationship to father is described as good. Mother
   feels he is not firm enough with her. He does not
   react to her behavior like mother does. Relationship
   to mother is tense. Mother feels that Emily's affection
   is full of hostility. Mother continually compares
   Emily unfavorably with her younger sister.

BEHAVIORAL OBSERVATIONS:
   Emily is a tall, slender girl with long brown hair.
   She did not greet the examiner, nor look at her. She
   played while her mother was interviewed in the

adjacent office, and the two separated without a word to each other.

During the testing, Emily began to draw rather than waiting for test instructions, indicating her need to be controlling. She liked to be praised, though she would not acknowledge it. When the examiner encouraged her to draw, she relaxed somewhat and became more cooperative. She began to smile and all of a sudden looked much prettier; even her dimples showed. Emily appeared sad but at the same time appealing.

TEST RESULTS AND INTERPRETATION:

Emily's measured IQ places her within a high range of cognitive functioning. She passed all tests on a five-year level and proceeded to the nine-year level. After she only passed one test at that age level, testing was discontinued as Emily reacted negatively to failure. Emily is quick to respond and shows strength in meaningful memory, language skills, and conceptual thinking.

Emily's Visual Motor Integration (VMI) score places her at the 5 year 4 months level. This is consistent with her mother's report that Emily's large motor development is slow. She is just now learning to pedal a tricycle. She has trouble hopping and balancing. Small motor skills are progressing, though she cannot zip and does not dress "very well." Emily struggles with pencil dexterity. She is consistently left-handed.

Emily's freehand drawings are age-appropriate. When asked to draw her family, she began at the right side of the paper by drawing Juliana first, then her mother, her dad, her baby brother, and, with some urging, herself. She placed the baby in her mother's arms.

It is significant that she drew her mother and father the same size as her sister. She drew herself much smaller, although she is nearly three years older. Undoubtedly, Emily sees herself as a lesser member of the family.

Emily elaborated, drawing a sun, a house, and a tall building. It is almost pathetic, however, that she needed to put a smiling countenance on the house, not only on the people and the sun. Despite the smiles, Emily's drawing looks sad.

Emily would not take the examiner's hand to walk to the kitchen, but she accepted a cookie.

It is recommended that Emily be seen in individual therapy at The Children's Center. She and her mother should also be seen in joint sessions to help develop a healthier relationship.

GROUP THERAPY

Group therapy.

Although I don't know it's called group therapy. All I know is that most of the days when I come to The Children's Center it's just Marsha and me, but today there are other kids here, and a bunch of "big people" I don't know.

Except Dr. John. I know Dr. John because he talks to my mom. I guess he talks to kids, too, because he's sitting at a long white table on a little chair like the kids'. I don't get why we're all here. I'm with six random kids and no Marsha. I want it to be the other way around. I tell Dr. John, "Usually when I come here there is Marsha and no kids, and today there are kids and no Marsha." This is the nicest way I can think of to say it.

"It's important we all talk together, not just kid-to-big-person but kid-to-kid, too."

He's wrong. Dr. John is wrong. I don't need to talk to other kids. I talk to kids all the time. I don't need The Children's Center for that.

"Plus we get to paint!" He raises his fist in a cheer, and I perk up. Big people start opening white cabinets and put color into the room a piece at a time.

We put giant smocks—blue plastic ones—over our clothes. They put poster paint on the counter. It is crusty around the edges, and it smells good, old and different and like faraway. The orange jar is almost empty. A pregnant lady a boy calls Pregnant Jill unrolls glossy white paper from a spool jutting out from a wall in the back. How did I not notice this earlier? It's beautiful, watching Pregnant Jill cutting us each a massive hunk of shiny paper.

If I had a roll of paper like that, I wouldn't cut it, though. I would leave it in one enormous strip. I'd start at the beginning and draw and write and paint and make one long story, and I would keep going until my story took over the entire house. My words and pictures would never stop.

Now, we sit at the white table, each with a place mat of white paper. Dr. John says: "I want you to paint a picture of the scariest thing that has ever happened to you."

A kid with a rattail says: "Monsters! No, aliens!"

Seriously? I wish I could give Rattail Kid a swift kick under the table, but I'm not sitting close enough. Instead I roll my eyes, obvious, so Dr. John can see.

"Monsters are scary," agrees a lady I don't know who has a scar on her arm that looks like a flower. "But we aren't just painting something scary. We're painting something scary that's real. Something that's scary because it happened to us. In real life. Does that make sense to you?"

Rattail Kid nods. He does not look like it makes sense to him.

I know right away what I'm going to paint, and not just because I like painting water. I reach for the blue paint before I'm supposed to, as a guarantee. No one says I can't or slaps my hand away, so I curl my fingers around the jar while Pregnant Jill goes over what we *won't* be doing while we paint: painting on ourselves or on other people, spilling the paint on purpose.

I paint the water one blue ribbon at a time, deeper and deeper. My brush makes the up-and-down swoops of the waves. I know the pool at Driftwood Park doesn't have waves like this, but that night it felt like it did. That night I was swimming with my family, but when I couldn't stand it anymore, when my brain was hurting too hard, I left them. I went deeper and deeper.

I couldn't touch. The water lapped over the crown of my head. I opened my eyes, but that made them sting, so I squeezed them shut again and held my breath. There was no sound. A moment earlier, there had been: hair metal band blasting from the red pickup in the visitor lot, people on their balcony yelling at each other, a TV turned too loud to a M*A*S*H rerun. Now nothing. Finally nothing. I didn't breathe. At first it scared me. Then it felt good not to breathe.

I add myself under the deepest ribbon. I am no more than a speck of brown paint.

Dr. John has us go around and talk about our artwork.

I think everything that has ever happened or ever will happen is the scariest thing for the girl next to me. I can't tell what she's painted, and every time the lady with the flower scar tries to get her to say something about it, she rolls up smaller into herself.

I kind of want to punch this girl. Dr. John sees my left hand clench and shoots me a glance like *Forget it*. Out loud, all he says is: "Your turn, Emily."

"This is the night I drowned," I announce, all eyes on me. "I was under the water. Couldn't touch the bottom. Couldn't touch the top. But then my dad came and pulled me out."

"I drowned once, too!" the scared girl exclaims, un-rolling. "I drowned, and it was so scary! I got rescued!"

Nods all around, from kids who drowned but were saved.

"It feels like drowning," says Dr. John. "But none of you actually drowned. When you drown, you go under-water, but you don't come back up."

He's wrong. Dr. John is wrong. I'm not like the other kids, the ones who think they've drowned but haven't. I have. The drowning's not what's below the water—it's what's above it.

THE CHILDREN'S CENTER

Emily Wing
Age: 6 years, 10 months
Therapists: John R. Starberger, LCSW, PhD
Jillian Beck, BS

GROUP THERAPY INITIAL REPORT

BEHAVIORAL OBSERVATIONS:
Emily is a pretty, brown-haired Caucasian girl
with freckles. She was hesitant to enter the group.
Eye contact was poor; she would initially drop her
head and avoid contact with other children or adult
therapists. Verbal communication was also limited
and consisted of short phrases spoken in almost a
whisper. Emily timidly asked for assistance during
snack or activities. Socially, Emily would play
beside, not with, another child. Little verbal or play
interaction occurred with peers. More often, Emily
engaged adults into conversation.

CLINICAL IMPRESSIONS:
Emily appears uncomfortable and uncertain of
herself in the outpatient group. She avoids verbal,
emotional, and, to a certain extent, physical contact
with her peers. She is less hesitant when interacting
with adults but is more interested in pleasing them

than in fulfilling her own autonomy or self-esteem needs. Verbal and physical outreach is difficult for Emily: She appears depressed and doesn't exhibit the physical energy, curiosity, or joy one associates with children her age.

TREATMENT GOALS:

1. Emily will increase verbal skills by making requests of other children and adults.
2. Emily will enter into and maintain cooperative play with peers for ten to fifteen minutes.
3. Emily will express feelings and initiate problem-solving skills.

"Emily is the oldest child. She has a younger sister, Juliana, and a baby brother."

GIVING ME A HEADACHE

I've always gotten headaches. I've gotten them for so long I was surprised to learn there were even such *things* as headaches—that headaches weren't the default setting for the human brain.

Sesame Street was over, and a cooking show had come on. A gray-haired lady was making pie using an old-fashioned apple corer. The apple corer didn't look like a kitchen tool; it looked like an instrument of torture: cold metal, a rod like a long screw that spun with a hand crank. She speared that shiny apple good, the apple flesh falling away from the rod, damaged. She started cranking.

My mom was on the couch, folding laundry and watching the baby. "That's like my head!" I told her. The rod in my head was always there, trying to crank out the brain matter between my temples. "My head feels like that apple." The feeling was the kind of pain that hurt so much it made me mad at everything and everyone, even though I knew that didn't make it okay to hit and stomp and throw things like I did.

"When you have that feeling, it's called a headache," Mom said. "Do you have a headache right now?"

When I had that feeling, it was called Wednesday. Of course I had a headache right now. I had a headache always.

And, with what I knew of life, that didn't surprise me.

THE SAFETY KIDS

Before we got the minivan, we had the white car. The white car had blue vinyl interior and an iffy air conditioner. We called it the white car so as not to confuse it with the yellow car, a pint-sized Rabbit with what we lovingly referred to as "the door that doesn't work" on the rear driver's side. When we drove the white car anyplace farther than school or church or the grocery store, we listened to *Safety Kids*.

The *Safety Kids* tapes had two volumes, one on general safety and one about staying safe from drugs. They also had workbooks so you could follow along and color the pictures if you got bored. The pictures were always scribbled in, but I never cared. Why should I have to color in pictures somebody else got to draw?

The Safety Kids were kind of tragic in the sense that you pretty much knew they were going to get beat up a lot.

There was Freddy, who spoke with an exaggerated lisp and always had one strap of his overalls undone. He inexplicably carried a frog in his pocket, and on most of the workbook pages the frog was front-row center, grinning in that way only cartoon frogs can. Amy was the Asian one. She had slits for eyes, so you couldn't color them in. Zan and Gregor were so generic I confused them. Monique was the boss.

The Safety Kids didn't bug me as much as they could have—some of their tunes were catchy. But for all their club meetings devoted to discussing safety, the Safety Kids knew very little about being safe. They sang about being "cautious of danger lurking anywhere," but it was a lie, because they didn't seem at all concerned that danger might be lurking just outside the abandoned shack where they had their meetings.

Everywhere is dangerous. Nowhere is safe.

The Safety Kids played by the rules. What they didn't tell you was that the rules don't help if the game is rigged.

SHELLEY'S HOUSE

It's the kind of summer that only exists when you're five years old and you don't know how long summer's supposed to be, when it could be June or July or August, but all you know is that summer has already been forever and might last until the rest of forever. Today Shelley says: "My mom and dad got a water bed."

Shelley lives on the other side of Driftwood Park, on the street past the playground where the ice-cream man drives. Shelley is not my friend, but it doesn't matter. It's summertime, and all the kids hang out together all day, every day. At Driftwood Park, if you aren't friends, you're enemies. You don't want enemies in a place like Driftwood Park.

My mom has told me not to go into Shelley's house. My mom says Shelley's dad is Not A Good Person, and even though I haven't met him, I believe it.

Shelley has a thick, bad smell on her that makes me choke and cough if she gets too close, and she wears jelly shoes with high-high heels and hoop earrings so big they brush her shoulders when she turns her head. Shelley never has to go in for dinner.

When the ice-cream man comes by, Shelley runs inside and always comes back with money, and the ice-cream man says, "Girl, do your parents know you're out here every day buying ice cream with another twenty-dollar bill?" And Shelley says her parents don't care. I've only ever once gotten to buy something from the ice-cream man, and when I tell my mom about how lucky Shelley is, about how every day she buys a Flintstones Push-Up with a twenty-dollar bill her parents give her, my mom says: "Emily, you are not allowed inside Shelley's house."

I play by the rules. I do not go inside Shelley's house. There's no reason to. Until one day, hot in summer, when Shelley announces her parents have a water bed.

Wide eyes and gasps all around. I've never heard of a water bed, but everybody else has. "It's a *water* bed," says Brandi. "Like a regular bed, but with water instead."

I picture an aquarium, like the one at my doctor's office. I imagine stretching out on a six-foot-long piece of glass and falling asleep to scenes of striped fish swimming behind seaweed. I hate trying to fall asleep, and counting fish seems much better than counting sheep.

"I want to see it," says Corey. He's older, the leader, the coolest kid in Driftwood Park. He is the only boy I've ever known with an earring—just one, small and silver.

"Me too," says everybody else, and Shelley, triumphant, leads the group, teetering on her high-heeled jellies.

Shelley's front door is locked during the day, not like mine; I go in and out anytime I want. Shelley wears a key on a silver chain around her neck. I think she should keep it out like a necklace, since she loves big jewelry, but Shelley says it's important to keep the key hidden. She tucks it under her tank top, but the outline shows through the ribs in the fabric.

When she unlocks the door, the smell escapes like it's been waiting for us—the thick, bad smell like on Shelley, only bigger. My eyes water and my throat closes up. Everyone else is doing fine. "This way," says Shelley, and they go in, but I turn away.

"Hurry up," says Brandi. She thinks I'm falling behind because I do that sometimes—get stuck imagining a story and stop talking and stop walking and freeze.

But this is not one of those times. I say, "I have to get home for lunch," and Brandi says lunch is over, and it is, so I say, "Dinner, then." And Chase says, "Yeah, right. What, are you afraid of drowning in the water bed?"

And the idea of drowning in the water bed had not occurred to me, but I'm not afraid, and I'm not about to let them peer-pressure me. I learned from *Safety Kids* that all you gotta say is no. So I say, "No!"

They give me a confused look and go inside, and I'm running. I'm running home because I play by the rules. Don't go in Shelley's house.

It doesn't happen in Shelley's house.

THE CHILDREN'S CENTER

Emily Wing
Age: 7 years, 4 months
Therapist: Marsha R. Blanche, PhD

CLINICAL IMPRESSIONS:

Emily was admitted into individual therapy at
The Children's Center after initial psychological
evaluation at age 6 years, 0 months. She has been in
individual therapy at The Children's Center since
January, for a total of 22 weekly sessions.

At 6 years, 10 months, Emily started group therapy.
Since that time, she appears to have made relatively
good progress but continues to have difficulty
expressing and recognizing feelings.

Emily's interactions with her sister are generally
appropriate and cooperative. But she occasionally
explodes into aggressive hitting and reports that: "I
need to do it. . . . I just have to hit her."

At the beginning of treatment, Emily felt it necessary
to bring an activity or a book with her, in an attempt
to structure the session and demonstrate that she
is a clever little girl and worthy of the therapist's
admiration. Emily gradually gave up this practice
and participated comfortably with the therapist in

activities geared toward helping Emily find ways to search for nonimpulsive solutions for her problems with members of her family. Emily used art, stories, and poems as preferred means to express her feelings. After using these techniques, Emily and her mother reported a decrease in impulsive behavior.

At discharge from individual therapy, Emily became more comfortable in communicating. However, her communications with her mother, while free of conflict at the present, represent an overanxiety to please, guilt over burdening the family or her mother with requests, and oversensitivity to gentle redirection. At such times, Emily apologizes, berates herself, and promises to do better.

It appears from therapists' reports and current data that Emily has made progress but has a tremendously high level of anxiety and continues to have difficulty coping on a day-to-day basis.

WATER BED

It happens at the playground, when I'm running away from Shelley's house and back to my house. When I get to the playground, I'm on my side of Driftwood Park, my home turf, where I'm safe, so I slow down. My legs burn in that way they burn only after I run, not while I run, and it makes me rethink ever stopping.

No one is at the playground. There's always someone at the playground. I never have the playground to myself, but right now everyone's at Shelley's, so I do.

My favorite place is a small cave underneath the slide, with a fireman pole on one side and a spiderweb of wiggly chains on the other. It is a small space, one I can't enjoy very often, because people are sliding down the fireman pole and climbing up the slide and jiggling the wiggly chains of the spiderweb, and all I can do in the small space is cover my ears and take up as little room as possible and pretend I'm somewhere else.

Today when I pretend I'm somewhere else, it's because that's what I want to do, not what I have to do, and I don't have to cover my ears. So I sit in the gravel and shape it into hills and ditches, and when I've gotten to the bottom of the gravel, once I've hit dirt, I start digging. My grandma says you can dig a hole to China. I don't believe that, because it doesn't make sense. But you must be able to dig to somewhere, and maybe there I can really be alone. My secret place.

I don't feel him watching me, so I flinch, startled, when I hear him laughing, and I look up and he's there. I've been making up a story, and sometimes when I do that, my characters talk to each other and I use different voices to tell them apart, and I forget to keep the voices in my head. Sometimes I sing without realizing it. I must have done one of those two things because he's not laughing *ha-ha* like I'm funny. He's laughing mean, like he caught me doing something wrong.

His name is Ken, or Kent, I can never tell which one when Corey calls his name: "Ken(t)! Get over here!" I don't have a reason to ask what his name is. He is old, maybe older than Corey, but it's hard to know for sure because all the almost-teenagers look the same to me.

Kent looks like Charlie in this movie I saw on TV a long time ago, *Willy Wonka and the Chocolate Factory*. I didn't like the movie, even though I got to stay up late to watch it. It made me sad how all of Charlie's grandparents had to share one bed. I wish they'd at least had a water bed so they could have looked at sea creatures while they were poor and sick and dying.

Willy Wonka creeped me out—I didn't like his top hat; I didn't like his eyes. Then Kent moved to Driftwood Park, and after that, Charlie creeped me out, too.

I hope to never watch that movie again.

"You're that weird girl, aren't you?" He says it like a question, but he knows the answer. He says it like he's daring me to disagree, making sure I know that everyone knows I'm the weird girl.

I do know I'm the weird girl. I've always known I was the weird girl.

"Have you seen one of these before?" Kent asks me, crouching down in my small space. A rectangle of yellow plastic with metal at one end, exactly the right size to fit into the palm of his hand; to only become visible when he uncurls his fingers. I have never seen one before. I get a feeling like I am going to regret this.

Kent smells bad, Shelley's-house-bad with a stripe of something sour. He folds his hand back over the yellow and turns his back. I should run, but I don't. I feel it all over: It is already too late.

He whirls around before I could have gotten any-where anyway. He whirls around like a magician, like he should be wearing a black cape lined in purple velvet. I half expect that, but no: He's still in his dirt-smudged red T-shirt.

The yellow stick is on fire now. One little flame. But I

know from being a Safety Kid, from learning not to play with matches, that one little flame is all it takes. One little flame can burn your house down.

"You know what this is, though, right?" I nod and he says, "I could burn up this whole playground if I wanted to. I could burn up both of us." I nod again. I wonder if he wants to.

Sometimes I wonder what it would feel like to be burned up. I know how it would feel at first. I've burned myself on a stove before, even though my mom said never to touch. The coil was almost back to black. I didn't believe it could still hurt me. When it did, I screamed and screamed.

The moment before the scream, though—it was just like the moment I'm in now. Paralyzed not with fright or pain, but with expectation: *It is already too late.*

When you finish burning, when there's no more pain, is there relief?

"Take off your pants," Kent says, and I wonder if he wants to burn them. "And take off your underwear."

"I don't wear underwear. I wear panties." Because I don't know there's no difference.

His laugh is dry, like he's thirsty. "Then take off your *panties.*" He narrows his eyes into slits, slits that curve like snakes. "And if you ever tell anyone, I will burn you. Then I'll burn your house." He waves the flame in front of me. "I'll burn your whole family."

THE CHILDREN'S CENTER

PSYCHOLOGICAL EVALUATION

Emily Wing
Age: 7 years, 10 months
Examiner: Mathew Cohen, PhD
Licensed Psychologist

TEST RESULTS AND INTERPRETATION:

Emily is a tall, slender Caucasian girl with long brown hair and freckles. She separated easily from her mother when approached by the examiner. Emily did not overtly respond when praised for successes, nor did she seem pleased with herself when she succeeded.

Most notable about Emily was her concern about drawing and the meticulousness with which she completed tasks of this nature. She appeared very anxious about doing well and being seen as a "good artist."

Emily's intellectual abilities remain consistent with previous evaluation, ranging between high average to superior cognitive functioning. On the Visual Motor Integration (VMI), Emily ranked in the fifty-fifth percentile, which is also consistent with previous findings. She was consistently left-handed.

—

Emily responded to questions in a pseudo-adult-like
fashion and used a great deal of intellectualization.
She seems to have a fairly clear idea of what she wants
to do when she grows up, which is illustrate books.
Although it is not unusual for a child this age to have
aspirations, Emily's delineation of what she needs to
do to obtain her goal seemed very clear-cut. Emily
does not appear to have an accurate appreciation of
her innate talents and skills, and struggles with using
overt behaviors to gain approval.

She seems to have a minimal perception of how
others see her, and this reflects continued difficulty
with self-esteem. Emily did not respond to inquiries
directed at feelings, and when this affect was
included in the response, it was usually "happy."
This seems to reflect some denial on Emily's part.

When asked to draw a person, she meticulously
drew a small figure at the bottom of the paper,
which she identified as a six-year-old girl running
to meet a friend. The figure was drawn in red and
heavily shaded, giving the impression of a great deal
of anxiety and low self-esteem. Emily appeared to
be quite anxious about doing well on this task and
overly concerned about obtaining approval for her

drawing. The orderliness and compulsivity of the drawing suggest Emily wards off inordinately high levels of anxiety through the use of avoidance and overinvolvement.

Given her progress in a group setting, it is recommended that Emily be discharged from The Children's Center. It is recommended, however, that Emily and her parents be encouraged to seek family therapy. Continued individual therapy may be considered if behavioral difficulties persist.

Looking pensive, preglasses.

GLASSES

I thought maybe I'd figured out what was wrong with me.

It was vision-screening day at my new school in Mid-valley, where my family moved last year. The students filed into the cafeteria/gymnasium like dominoes, each class in a line that funneled into one main line. Everyone took a turn covering one eye and reading. People cheated, peeking between fingers, so the volunteer moms had to cover them for us. It was quick and efficient.

Our volunteer was Bryan Wadsworth's mom. As I inched to the front of the line and watched the kids ahead of me, my panic set in. They read this big white poster hanging above the thick black out-of-bounds line on the gym floor.

The poster looked like the one we used at program

practice. At program practice, the entire second grade met in one classroom, and we all had to sit boy-girl, almost touching but not, and keep arms, legs, and other objects to ourselves while we learned songs for our Just Say No! performance. The words to the songs were on a poster, and I was too far back to read them, but I already knew the words because they were *Safety Kids* songs, and I was a Safety Kid from way back.

I thought: *What if this time I'm too far back? What if this time I don't know the words?*

Bryan Wadsworth's mom covered my eye with a lemon-scented hand. "Relax," she said. "Read the letters."

I could read, of course. I read at a who-knows-what-grade level. On a page, letters combined like geese in perfect formation, never questioning why they flew together. But these letters were nothing like letters on a page. Just black shoe-polish scuffs on a field of white. Only one real letter, an *E*, was at the top of a mountain of marks.

I told this to Bryan Wadsworth's mom. I said: "I only see one letter. An *E*."

She did not say what I longed to hear. She did not say: *That's right! Long or short E sound?* She made a small, sad sound instead. "Nothing else?" I'd disappointed her. I hated disappointing her. I didn't want her to feel my tears on her hand, so I tried not to cry. Trying not to cry has always made me cry.

Usually I was good at tests with letters and words, extra good. It made up for being extra bad at other things. But this test had letters and words, and I still failed. I still failed

in front of Bryan Wadsworth's mom. "I know how to read,"
I said, a sniffle.

She wiped away one of my tears, took her hand from
my eye. She had long, curly hair. Her smile was nicer than
Bryan Wadsworth's, and she said: "Emily, of course you
can read—what you can't do is see!" A joke, but it made me
cry harder.

I realized: *What if I look at everything everyone else looks
at and I see something different? What if it's never been any other
way?* That would explain it, wouldn't it? Why life was always different for me, always blurred edges?

At my appointment, the doctor told me that now, with
glasses, I'd be able to see the faraway words I never could
before. He said my eyes wouldn't have to strain to see and
it would take the pressure off. He asked me if I got headaches, and I said yes, and he said maybe now I wouldn't;
maybe now the pain would go away.

Later, my dilated eyes wide behind dark glasses with
thick cardboard frames, I watched the road and stared at
the signs I didn't know I was supposed to be able to read.
I touched the stiff frames, imagining the ones I'd have in
about an hour. I thought about how the lenses had made
tight everything that was loose, how they fixed things.

I thought maybe I'd be all better now.

With glasses. Maybe I am all better now?

ANT FARM

I get baptized because of ant farms and Old Bones.

My second-grade school year is still new enough that Juliana and I go to bed before the sun does. The almost-dark casts strange shadows over my sister's sleeping face. Outside our window, the clouds shift and the shadows chug away like a train.

Juliana always falls asleep first. She sleeps on the daybed, with white wrought-iron curlicues lulling her into the dream world that comes so naturally for her.

I sleep on Old Bones. It's what we call the trundle that I pull out every night from underneath the daybed. No one knows what might have happened to Old Bones to make her coils lump and bulge like they do, but it is clear to me she's had a tough life. Sleeping on Old Bones feels like lying on a malnourished woman's rib cage, which is how she got her name. I don't mind sleeping on her. Old Bones feels like a punishment I deserve, even though I don't know what I did yet.

When I don't sleep, which is nearly all the time, I have a game called Nobody Loves Me. The storyline to Nobody Loves Me changes nightly, but it always involves me taking off all my clothes and lying in the middle of the bedroom while I imagine the setup.

Sometimes my mother and father have died, and our house has been ransacked by thieves and burned to the ground, and now I must find my own way in the cold, bitter world. Sometimes my mother has been kidnapped, and my stepmother hates me and has forced me out to live in the snowy woods by myself. Sometimes I wake up one day and my parents are gone, and there is no more heat and I must find some way to get warm.

Then I roll under the daybed and I make a cave for myself, and when I start to shiver, I pretend I've been adopted by a nice family of moles who live underground, or mutant people who've been shunned from society, or a group of cheerful, hardworking orphans, and I crawl into bed and fall asleep.

But tonight it is still September, and it won't get cold enough for Nobody Loves Me, so I pull my nightgown back over my head and do what I do when the game doesn't work, which is worry. This creepy in-between shade of night is prime for worrying.

I am almost eight years old. Eight years old means I can be baptized if I want to, that I can go underwater and my sins can be washed away. I can take the name of Jesus Christ upon me, and I can join the Church of Jesus Christ of Latter-day Saints and receive the Holy Ghost. I can devote my life to Heavenly Father, and I want to.

But I have seen my future if I stay in this church, and it is not good.

"Ants are stronger than humans," Matt B. says to me. "Ants can carry up to fifty times their body weight." Matt B. likes to talk about what he knows.

I'm not even looking at the ant farm. I'm just waiting for a drink at the classroom drinking fountain. But Matt B. brought the ant farm in for show-and-tell on the second day of school, and it's ended up staying here on the back counter indefinitely.

"They have bigger brains than we do, too. I mean, for their size." Matt B. is the one kid in this class who is possibly liked less than I am, and it is in no small part because he is in second grade and uses phrases like *for their size.* "Ants are better than humans in most ways."

I'm not arguing.

Josh, the kid ahead of Matt B., yells to Bryan, "Save some for the fish!" and the kids back at their seats laugh. Bryan keeps gulping.

From the outside, watching from the safe side of the glass, all the ants look the same. Small on their own, believing that together they'll make something bigger, so they do. Together they build an intricate, sophisticated home for themselves. It makes me think of church, even though I know ant farms wouldn't make normal kids think of church.

I never know why something makes me think of something else. I asked my dad once, and he told me it's called a train of thought, and everybody has one, even normal kids. But my thoughts are a runaway mine train, like the ride at Disneyland. With normal kids, one thought leads to another, everything linked up and led by a conductor named Mr. Brain. My thoughts have no conductor, only train cars starting together and splitting apart and praying they stay on the rails.

So I think of ants like people in church, worker ants that all look the same. From the outside, I look just like one of the almost-eight-year-old girl ants, with a church dress and tights and poufy bangs. But everyone on the inside knows that I am not like them. My dress is wrinkled and my tights are on backward and my bangs are only poufed on one side because getting my hair curled makes my head hurt and I always run away before my mom can finish. I am the weird girl. I am the backward girl. I am not the right girl.

"Dude, save some for the fish!" Brent, a kid who's not even in line, calls out from his desk. It's not funny the second time, but the rest of the class thinks it is and laughs again. Matt B. gives a wannabe laugh, but I can't even manage that.

I don't want to give wannabe laughs. I don't want poufy bangs. But I want to be a worker ant. I want to build Heavenly Father's kingdom on Earth because I believe. I do.

Sometimes the blood in my body is so thick with pain

and worries and ideas it's as if it stops moving. And in moments like that, when I can't breathe or move or think straight, all I know is that something horrible is about to happen; I just don't know what yet. Those times, Heavenly Father pushes the *on* button inside me, and I know it was Him because no one else can reach it.

From the outside, none of the ants look any different from the others, any faster than the others, any slower than the others. None of them are in the corner, stopped, all the blood inside them frozen as the pain and terror and confusion of living leaves them stunned. From my side of the glass, I will never know if one of them, with its huge brain, is thinking, *Wait! Can't any of you see I'm not like you? That every single day I'm building this beautiful, intricate kingdom, but part of me wonders if there's even room for me inside it?*

An ant gets caught in the sand. It is only for a moment, and Matt B. is looking at the other ants working without a hitch, following all the others, putting on an act for us on the safe side of the glass: *Look at what we've made. Just look at it. Flawless.*

Matt B. sits back to enjoy the show.

But even from the safe side of the glass, I hear it from the lips the caught ant doesn't have. I hear the caught ant: *HELP.*

I put out my finger, try to touch his *on* button through the glass. But there is nothing I can do.

Tonight, Old Bones squeaks as I roll off her and under the daybed, making a cave for myself. I crouch in a half-kneel and ask God. I put it all out there, even though I know He already knows. About the poufy bangs and the tights and how the other kids don't care about Him like I do, how they'd rather make fun of me because I haven't seen *E.T.*, and why does that even matter? About how I love Him. About how I'm not sure I love the Church, but if He wants me to, I will.

And I hear Him.

God has never spoken to me before, although at church, in Primary, we learn how to listen for Him. Some people get a burning in their heart, or a warm feeling all over, and His spirit speaks in a still, small voice. It's different for everyone, they say, and hard to describe. Which is obvious from their lack of description. What sound would a still, small voice even make? Because by definition, sound isn't still, and the kind of volume you can hear isn't measured in size.

But when God talks to me, I know exactly what everybody means, because I hear Him in words I'm not sure He utters or I simply feel. But there is no mistaking it: *Join the Church. You won't be sorry.*

And I've been sorry, it seems, since before I was born, that even in utero I knew there was something not quite right about me. *Sorry, Mom, to be the one coming first. Sorry that you have to practice on the hardest one. Sorry that you can't start with the right girl, one who can sleep through the night or ride a bike, who knows how to make friends and be safe and not need an* on *button pushed. Sorry. Sorry. Sorry.*

And all I know is that if God's giving me one less thing to be sorry about, I'll take it.

LEFTY

Learning to write is harder than it should be.

Not learning to put words on paper and make them stories. That part comes familiar, as natural as dreaming. Once I write my first sentence, I forget there was ever a time I didn't.

But leading up to that first sentence . . . It's like the other kids were born knowing how to hold a pencil. Our kindergarten teacher shows us once and goes around and moves our fingers into place. I see the recognition on their faces: *Oh, this feels right.* To me it feels so, so wrong, and as soon as Teacher turns her back, I hold it the way I think I should, in a death grip.

I do worksheets, tracing the letters of the alphabet, and they always come out dark and smudged and looking nothing like real letters. Teacher knows I'm careful, so she watches me. She rotates my hand so I see the side of it that hits the paper when I write. A silver streak runs from my pinkie to my wrist.

"You're a lefty," she says, "so you need to do this differently."

I'm a lefty, so I have to do everything differently. Especially because I'm extra left-handed.

Most people can use their left hand okay and their right hand better. I assume it's the opposite for regular left-handers: they can use their right hand okay but their left hand better. But my left hand isn't just better—it's extra better. It's so much better I barely use my right hand at all. I call it Bad Hand. It's been Bad Hand since always.

My dad has told me left-handers are more creative, more artistic. He's said artists spend time in their own mind, living in a world all their own. My mom has told me artists are more high-strung. She's said they're quicker to get frustrated and lash out.

I'm extra creative, extra artistic. I spend extra time in my own mind, living in a world all my own. I'm extra high-strung, extra quick to get frustrated and lash out. I've been this way since always.

My parents tell me left-handers are special, different. I've been extra different since always.

So I have to write extra differently.

I practice holding my pencil, and it practices not working. It becomes perfect. I don't.

I should be able to write. I'm a smart girl. I do smart like I do everything: extra. I'm not like Timothy or Misty, who can't write because they don't know how to read, don't even know the letters or what sound they make. In my mind, I can see exactly how each word is supposed to look.

My worksheets come home crumpled, wrinkled from dried tears.

I have so many words inside me that I want a piece of paper to hear.

Why can't my hand keep up?

After too long, after too many tears, after it's clear to all involved parties that I could write if only my hand would cooperate, the grown-ups give in. I'm allowed to hold my pencil a third way. Not my death grip. Not the way everybody else does. A hybrid of what they've always told me is right and what they've always told me is wrong.

It's the first time I understand compromise. It won't be the last.

With this third way, my fingers curl without the need to push so hard. My pencil lead doesn't break. My hand still turns silver on the side, but the words aren't smudged. And finally, *finally*, my letters look like real letters. My mind is off and running, and my hand keeps up.

And this teacher says, "Well, whatever works."

And I think, yeah, whatever *does* work.

Seascape, second grade.

WATER BED REVISITED

"Mom?" I ask. She is washing dishes. I am on the floor, painting with my new acrylics. They are artist-grade acrylics, bought with the money I got for my eighth birthday at the university bookstore. I could only afford three tubes. I wanted a perfect, intricate shade called Camellia Rose, but I got red, yellow, and blue instead. With those I can make my own Camellia Rose. I'm not making Camellia Rose today, though. Today, I am painting water.

"Yes?"

"Are you and Dad ever going to get a water bed?"

"Dad and I don't want a water bed," Mom says. "Where did you hear about a water bed?"

"Shelley's parents had one," I tell her. "You know, at Driftwood Park? Don't worry, I didn't go see it." I want her to know how hard I try to play by the rules.

That's why I haven't told her about Kent, even though we're safe now, even though we've moved to our very own house in Midvalley, far away from Driftwood Park. In our very own house in Midvalley, light from the kitchen window washes in over my mother and me. Only I still know what I've always known: Nothing like Kent would have happened to the right girl. To a not-weird, not-backward girl. I wish I could make her believe I'm the right girl.

"I wanted to see the water bed, though. I still want to see a water bed." Today I paint the water in squares, teeny-tiny squares, each a darker shade of blue. "I want my own water bed."

"You don't even sleep in the bed you have now," my mom says.

But we go to a big furniture showroom that weekend, to buy our first real dining room table, and my parents say I can go see the water beds if, when I finish, I follow the signs straight back to KITCHEN AND DINING. So I follow the signs to BEDS AND MATTRESSES and can't find what I'm looking for. I ask a salesman in a too-bright tie, and he points to it. The bed frame is wooden, not glass like I expected, so I have to peek over to look inside.

And it is the saddest thing because there are no fish and no sea creatures and no water, not really. The water bed is just a king-sized balloon of a mattress that feels like it's filled with warm jelly, like it could explode at any second.

JOHANNA

Johanna was the first friend I made already knowing she was out of my league. We were in third grade, and I fell in love with her during an episode of *3-2-1 Contact.*

Johanna was smart, like I was, but unlike me, she was the kind of smart you didn't notice, because she was normal, too. She hung out with Kacie and Jess, the popular girls in class. At recess, they circled our portable classroom, sauntering casually but territorially. We watched them from our tetherball poles and four-square courts and shot them looks that said: *Don't worry. We know who's boss.*

Even before I knew her, I knew Johanna wasn't like them. I could tell by the way she walked, with her shoulders semi-slumped, and the way her bangs were never curled and fluffed and sprayed like theirs. Her bangs were too long and straight, like mine.

Mrs. Elkins moved our desks next to each other. Kacie and Jess were together, too, but on the other side of the room. We had science in the afternoon, and Mrs. Osborne dimmed the lights and popped a tape into the VCR. *3-2-1 Contact* bored me 99 percent of the time. I always wondered if secretly the topics interested everyone else and it was just another way I wasn't right.

This episode was devoted to kelp.

Kelp, it turned out, was an unheralded hero. This sea plant was used in making everything the modern consumer enjoyed—from ice cream to toothpaste. On and on about the wonders of kelp.

And I don't remember which one of us said it: "Next thing you know, they'll be telling us about kelp spaghetti."

"Kelp nail polish remover."

"Kelp Pepto-Bismol."

"Kelp peanut butter."

On and on about the wonders of kelp.

Mrs. Elkins said, "Whoever is whispering must *stop!*" We did, because we played by the rules.

I didn't want to push my luck, so I didn't. I still stayed away at recess, and I didn't smile at her or look at her or act like it meant anything. We weren't friends—couldn't be—not in the third-grade world we lived in. I played it cool because even I knew playing it any other way would be social suicide.

Still, we thought ourselves quite clever that day. And I couldn't remember ever having so much fun, or feeling like someone felt the way I did.

Dyeing eggs with Dad.

THE MEDALLIONS

Writing is like art, only better.

We have a framed collage-style picture hanging over the light switch in my parents' bedroom. It isn't on the main level, where everyone would be able to see it, and I know it's because the pictures are only of me and Dad and Mom. It was long ago, before Dad refused to get his picture taken. The rest of our family didn't exist yet.

In my favorite picture, I'm kneeling on a kitchen chair next to Dad. He has a mustache, but otherwise he looks like he should. We're dyeing Easter eggs. I loved punching the egg-shaped holes out of the cardboard carton where the eggs sat to dry. I remember setting my egg in the cup of blue and then getting impatient and moving it into green, and I never kept them in long enough for the cheap, diluted dye to stick. I couldn't figure out why my eggs didn't turn the color of the dye I put them in.

In the picture I'm happy. I know because I've never been able to fake a plausible smile. But I'm sure I lost it. As soon as Dad ladled the egg from the mug, pasty white and shedding tinted water like a kid fresh out of a swimming pool, I bet I went nutso.

What I see in my mind has never quite matched what I see in reality. Until I learn to write.

Once I figure out how to hold my pencil, I can write any words I want, and they can make my idea look any way I want it to. I can add more blue or more green by changing words to *sapphire* or *emerald*. Words never let me down. With words, I never let myself down.

Fourth grade is lonely. At the time, I don't realize the feeling as loneliness. I feel it as every other emotion: Boredom, because I'm not challenged. Annoyance, because the other kids are idiots. Rage, because there's always been this part of me that loses it and goes nutso when I'm bored and annoyed and lonely. Everything swirls together to make rage. I pick fights with Juliana, and I can get out a slap or a kick or an arm-twist before I'm sent to my room.

I'm in my room a lot. Sometimes because I'm sent there and I have to count to ten and punch my pillow, things that never make me any less angry. But then I stay there. I stay there so much that Mom lets me swap rooms and share with my baby brother, who sleeps most of the time, so I can be almost-alone.

Almost-alone in my room, I write volume one of The Medallions.

The Medallions is a series of wide-ruled–spiral-bound–notebook-length books about four preteen girlfriends: ringleader Nissia, beautiful and mysterious Cassandra, bookish Meghan, and free-spirited Hana.

The girls attend the elite West Carriford Academy in LA. Students take classes in pottery and photography and astronomy instead of spelling and fractions and long division. They row crew for sport and have never heard of playing broom hockey in a dusty cafeteria/gym.

When a rival group shows up, threatening to take over the school with their matching barrettes and catty put-downs and general Mean Girl spirit, the four band together to form The Medallions—an equally cliquish club, but one based on love. The girls earn their namesake medallions by reading to nursing-home residents, giving toys to needy children at Christmas, and otherwise fixing Los Angeles one medallion at a time.

They have fun, too, of course. It's always a subplot. First and foremost, I want readers to know how interesting and smart and generous The Medallions are, how much they value social responsibility. The Medallions are the kind of girls who have friends, who make them without even trying, and they know they're lucky. But they're not stuck-up; they don't think their popularity means anything. The Medallions are clever and they study hard and they help others, like you should if you are blessed with the ability to have friends.

It's with their leftover time that they get ice-cream sodas at their hangout, Henderson's, and make plans.

They shop for fantastic outfits (like Cassandra's tan jumpsuit with safari-print shirt and matching fedora). They throw elaborate parties, like a New Year's Eve bash including streamers, poppers, hats, and confetti (all silver, their signature color) as well as root beer, Sprite, Pepsi, *and* Coke (because it's a special occasion). They go camping and roast hot dogs and marshmallows and sing camp songs (with words I get to make up, because I'm writing the story).

They have sleepovers in their matching silver-and-purple sleeping bags, and they order pizza and talk about the dumb/cute boys at school, and they sleep four in a row.

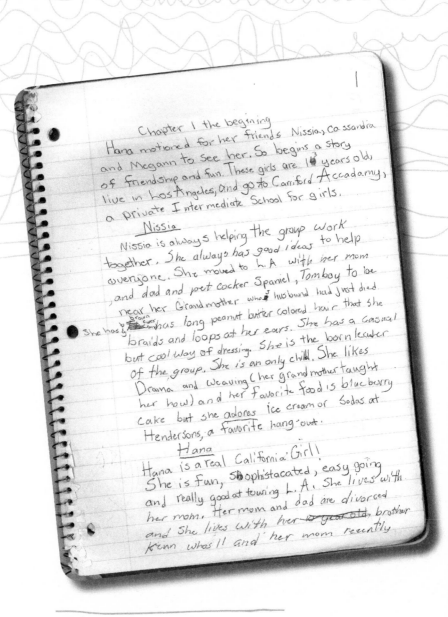

Chapter 1 the begining

Hana motioned for her friends Nissia, Cassandra and Megann to see her. So begins a story of friendship and fun. These girls are 13 years old, live in Los Angeles, and go to Carnford Accadamy, a private Intermediate School for girls.

Nissia

Nissia is always helping the group work together. She always has good ideas to help everyone. She moved to L.A with her mom and dad and pet cocker Spaniel, Tomboy to be near her Grandmother whose husband had just died. She has brown long peanut butter colored hair that she has long peanut butter colored hair that she braids and loops at her ears. She has a casual but cool way of dressing. She is the born leader of the group. She is an only child. She likes Drama and Weaving (her grandmother taught her how) and her favorite food is blueberry cake but she adores ice cream or sodas at Hendersons, a favorite hang-out.

Hana

Hana is a real California Girl! She is fun, sophisticated, easy going and really good at touring L.A. She lives with her mom. Her mom and dad are divorced and she lives with her 10 year old brother Kenn whos 11 and her mom recently

---

THE MEDALLIONS, fourth grade.

HOW IT DOESN'T HAPPEN

Here is how it doesn't happen: I don't calmly give my mom a detailed account of what went down with Kent, including his last name and an accurate physical description. We don't call the police, and justice isn't served. It doesn't happen like it should, the way it would unfold in a *Safety Kids* tape.

I don't plan to tell her. The older I get, the more ashamed I am that I even let it happen, that I didn't run away before he could catch me, or hide somewhere he was too big to fit, or yell loud enough that maybe someone would hear me through their window screen. But I didn't do any of that. Why not? Was I stupid enough to believe he would burn up my family? Did I secretly want it to happen?

The story comes out one night when I'm in my room throwing one of my signature rages, sobbing so hard I can already feel my veins popping out. A headache this bad while I'm still crying does not bode well for what's to come once I stop, and that makes me cry harder. I'm a fourth grader, too old for tantrums, but I'm the only one who seems to realize that these aren't tantrums. My rages are all that keep me from crawling into a ball, taking up as little space as possible, and staying that way until my life is over.

How it happens is a blur: My mom comes in demanding to know what's wrong *this* time. I tell her how everything hurts. How everyone at school hates me, how I want to punch them or kick them so I can make them feel pain instead of them making me feel pain. I don't know what makes me add: "And how am I supposed to be like other kids after what happened to me?" My mom says: "What happened to you?" Even though I brought it up, I didn't mean to, so I don't know what to say, and my words don't follow one another in a logical order or even make sense, and it's a runaway mine train of thought spewed out onto my mother, who looks sometimes confused, sometimes sad, sometimes sympathetic—like a mom in a picture book.

She says she had no idea. She says she'll call Driftwood Park to see if Kent still lives there. She'd put me in therapy, but I'm already *in* therapy—I see Dr. John sometimes at his private office downtown. She says she'll try to move up my next appointment. I imagine this checking off yet another box on my long list of mental health issues. I imagine Dr. John thinking, *Yep, saw this coming.*

Before Mom leaves the room, once I've stopped heaving and am back to breathing, she touches my knee. "Is there a possibility that Ken or Kent might have done something like this to Juliana?"

"Juliana?" Why would he hurt Juliana? She's not the weird girl. Kent chose me because he knew I was broken to begin with. Kent chose me because I had a target on my back.

How I remember Juliana that summer: blond. A little shy but smiley. Three and a half. Not broken. No target.

"Nothing happened to her," I say. When I say it, I know it's true, a truth Juliana confirms later. "No. Juliana's safe."

DR. JOHN'S

I think I'm supposed to like Dr. John more than I do.
My mom loves Dr. John. She's always quoting things he's told her in one of their sessions. But something about Dr. John feels off to me. Maybe it's that something about me feels off to Dr. John.

"Your mom wanted us to start meeting regularly again," says Dr. John. He looks like a caricature, with a big face and a teeny-tiny body. "Why do you think that is?"

"She didn't tell you?" My mom sees Dr. John more often than I do. I assumed he already knew. I was counting on it.

"I want to hear about it from you."

Of course he does. *He* doesn't have to relive that day at the playground. The story doesn't ride the teeter-totter between embarrassing and terrifying for *him*.

"Umm, could we talk about something else first?" I try not to whine. If I can buy some time, I can write it out like a story in my mind. I can work out the kinks, and when I recite it back to him, there won't be any important details missing and no extra parts that don't matter.

"Sure," he says. "What do you want to talk about?" I haven't come up with an alternative subject, and he must be able to tell, because he says smoothly, "Or we could play a game, if you want."

I think he means some weird psych game, with ink-blot pictures and word associations, but he means Guess Who?

We sit in the corner of the room, at a table too short for us, and we set up the board game. Rows of illustrated faces stare up at me from the tray, bland and unassuming. They want nothing from me. I haven't let them down. It's such a relief.

I win the first game in no time, because Dr. John's mystery person is Maria, and there are only a few females to choose from in the sea of men that is Guess Who? He says we can play again, and I'm determined to take as long as possible. I'm not ready to give my statement yet.

"Is your person wearing a hat?" He gets to go first because he lost last time.

"Nope. Is your person Max?" If I guess one mystery person at a time, I can drag this out as long as I need to.

Dr. John shakes his head. "No. Does your person have a big nose?"

I nod, and he raises his eyebrows and smiles. On his

tray, Dr. John flips down mystery face after mystery face.

"Hmm . . ." I scan my tray. One of the faces looks just like Dr. John's. "Is your person Paul?"

Dr. John's eyebrows fall. "How did you know? Did you see my card?"

"What? Your mystery person is really Paul?"

He turns his tray to face me. His mystery person is really Paul. "I promise, I did not see your card."

"I know. You wouldn't cheat." Dr. John looks amazed. "You've always been like this. So smart. Seriously, how did you figure it out?"

"Are you letting me win?" I ask. I'm almost eleven. He doesn't need to let me win.

"How do you let someone win at Guess Who?" He has a point. "You've always been like this," he says again, and I don't know what he means. I hold my breath. "So smart," he finishes.

I pick up the loose yellow-backed cards of mystery faces, using my left hand to straighten them into a pile. I keep my head down. "You know how I've always been like this?"

"Smart?" he asks, like he knows that isn't it.

"Weird. Different. Wrong."

I expect him to say what he's supposed to say, the lies that are part of his doctor oath, that I'm not weird or different or wrong. But he doesn't say anything, so I keep talking. "Do you think this is why? Because of what happened? Because I was, you know, abused?"

Maybe the headaches and the Bad Hand and the weird

girl and the rages—maybe it's all because of this. Maybe I can tell Dr. John the story I've rehearsed in my head and he can help me process and, voilà—I'll be healed. The curse will be lifted. "Maybe you can make me all better." It's an accident that I say it out loud.

"Em," he says, "no one can make you all better except for yourself."

His words fall on me like slivered glass and sink into my skin, more painful with each second that passes. Because I've tried to make myself all better—I have. And I know it like you know it when you're getting a sunburn: If no one can make me all better except for myself, then I don't stand a chance.

POSITIVE ACTION

One of the lamer aspects of my elementary school education is a program called Positive Action. Each grade level has a corresponding workbook on how to build character and a healthy self-concept.

I hate self.

By fifth grade, Positive Action is largely an independent activity. Mrs. Manwaring assigns pages, and everyone else scribbles fill-in-the-blank answers quick, between science and last recess. It takes me longer. "What did you put for number three?"

Dirk looks up at me. He has the characteristics of a firstborn fawn. His skin is tanned, and his eyes are olive green. His hair is light on the top, like straw, and dark on the bottom, like wet sand. "Um . . . basketball."

"You can't copy," says Kimmy from three desks

down. I have not asked Kimmy on purpose. Every class has a Kimmy, all up in everyone's business. She even looks the part, with a pointy nose and mousy-brown hair that swishes behind her whenever she shakes her head con-descendingly. Kimmy says: "You shouldn't copy on any-thing, but you *especially* can't copy on Positive Action."

She's right, of course. The question is: *What trait or skill do I have that I can develop as my personal trademark?*

I ask Dad for homework help that night. The Nintendo is in front of him, the cord splayed like yarn after a kitten's chased it. He's playing *The Legend of Zelda*, but he can do two things at once. When I tell him I need help with Posi-tive Action, he says he doesn't know what that is but okay.

I start with the limerick I'm supposed to write on what I can do to feel good about myself. I'm a good writer, but I'm not great at poetry. As much as a limerick can be called poetry. Everything I think to write sounds stupid.

Dad makes up rhymes, but I think he doesn't under-stand the question.

> *When people say my dad is weird*
> *When it's everything I've ever feared*
> *I say, "I know my dad's odd*
> *But he has a great bod*
> *A mustache and a bright blue beard."*

"I like that one." He's smiling and pleased with him-self, pressing the red *B* button repeatedly.

"But it isn't the assignment, Dad."

"It's good, though. It's creative."

I sigh, winding the Nintendo cable around my hand like a glove. "Let's skip to the other one. 'What trait or skill do I have that I can develop as my personal trademark?'"

He says, "Read it again?" and I do, and for a few seconds I think he wasn't listening the second time, either, because all he's doing is buying some potion and not answering. Finally he says: "If I were you, I'd write: 'I disagree with this approach.'"

So I write, *I disagree with this approach*, and that's how I handle Positive Action after that.

There are no letter grades for Positive Action. On the report card, it's in the same section as art and PE. The teacher checks a box for each one. Either SATISFACTORY or NEEDS IMPROVEMENT.

And I know that Mrs. Manwaring likes me. I know it isn't personal, that she's only doing it because I filled up an entire page of the Positive Action workbook with a story about a group of friends who spend the summer driving an ice-cream truck. But still, it hurts to see it.

POSITIVE ACTION: NEEDS IMPROVEMENT.

MELISSA'S HOUSE

I've never been the kind of girl who responds to treatment. Therapy didn't make me normal. Glasses didn't get rid of my headaches. I am not surprised and I am not scared.

There is only one time I am scared, on a Friday night at the end of fifth grade.

I am sleeping over at Melissa's house. I sleep over at Melissa's all the time. Melissa and I are neighbors and are in the same Girl Scout troop, and it's an easy, simple friendship.

It's the exact opposite of my friendship with Johanna. Or, you know, "friendship" with Johanna. At the beginning of the year, she broke it off with Kacie and Jess, and no one knows why, but I saw my chance. Mrs. Manwaring sat Johanna and me at the same table, and when the class changed desks two months later, we were still at the same table. And little by little, I'm growing on her, like kelp on the ocean floor. Sometimes we'll be talking before recess and it continues as we walk out to recess and then recess is happening and we're still talking and I'm hanging out with Johanna! At recess!

All week, I cultivate our friendship by saying witty things and laughing at the right time and not laughing at the wrong time. I know I'm lucky to have the chance to prove myself. But by the weekend, I'm exhausted. By the weekend, I want to not think and not watch myself and not worry if I sound stupid and just relax with Melissa.

Melissa's mom, Debbie, is one of our troop leaders. I feel like I should call her Sister Kendell because she's also in my ward at church. But she wants me to call her Deb, so I compromise and call her Sister Deb.

Sister Deb likes me. I can impress Sister Deb without even trying. I read her the stories I write, with expression and voices, and she laughs at the right places and gasps at the right places and claps at the end. I know she thinks I'm funny in a way she doesn't think other kids are funny.

Once, Sister Deb told me about a guy on TV who could bend a spoon just by concentrating on it hard enough. The spoon bent in his hand easy, like a pipe cleaner. "I bet you could do that, too," she said. "With all that brainpower you have." We got a spoon out of the silverware drawer, and Melissa and her two little sisters watched me chant: "Bend, spoon, bend." The spoon bent in my hands easy, like a pipe cleaner, and it turned out the spoon was weak, that even

Melissa's little sisters could bend it, but I never forgot how Sister Deb thought I could do it first.

Melissa has two cats, Sam and Tuna. I'm allergic to them, but I sleep over there anyway and take Benadryl before we snuggle into beds made from her Care Bears comforter and the itchy, crocheted blankets on the couch. Tonight we watch *Carousel*, an old musical that Sister Deb loves. It bores me. Lots of movies bore me. I like the stories I make up better.

Sam and Tuna must be shedding more than usual, because tonight it's not just my face feeling the pressure; it's my whole head. It's like all my insides from the neck up are swelling. It hurts and I'm bored.

Sometimes I sneak out of the family room and read books while the movie finishes up. Melissa likes Nancy Drew, not The Baby-Sitter's Club like I do, but she has the Little House books, so I read those over and over.

This time, I creep down the hall as usual, but before I get to Melissa's room, my feet slip out from under me. Not a normal trip-and-fall slip out from under me, either. My head is spinning, and my legs feel like they were never there to begin with.

And this is not because Sam and Tuna are shedding more than usual. This isn't allergies. This isn't a new degree of my ever-present headache. This is something else entirely.

I'm near the bathroom, so I slither onto the cool linoleum that they laid just last year. Lying on the floor, I can see the places that never get cleaned—the corner between the sink and the wall where there's fur and dried tooth-paste and hairballs.

I try to stand, but halfway up, I fall back down.

Then I throw up.

I hardly ever throw up. It's only happened two other times that I can remember. Once when I had the chicken pox and once when I had the flu. I slept in Mom and Dad's bed because it was closest to the toilet. I didn't want anything to eat, not even chicken-and-stars soup.

But this isn't like being sick. I don't feel that churning in my stomach—I don't feel anything in my stomach. I don't know it's coming. It just happens.

What's happening to me? *Woozy*. The word comes into my mind like it's always been there, though I don't remember ever using it before. I have a woozy headache. A headache, but something more. Pain and pressure, but dizziness and weakness, too.

I lie there, waiting for the spinning in my head to stop, waiting for my woozy-head to go away. Periodically I roll from side to side to keep each cheek cool. The head-throbbing slows down to its usual head-throbbing speed. Then I get up and start cleaning. Sister Deb can't see this.

A bleary-eyed Melissa comes in. She flips on the light and starts blinking, and the fluorescent light also starts blinking, and she says, "Em, did you just barf?"

This kind of barf is not something you can deny. I wish I could. I'm eleven years old. I'm old enough to be able to get to the toilet, old enough to be able to aim, old enough not to spew all over the bathroom floor at someone else's house. And Sister Deb. Sister Deb likes me and my stories and my brainpower. I can't ruin that.

And deeper down, this moment is adding one more moment to the knot of fear I've nursed for as long as I can remember. The fear made up of moments showing me I'm not right. The fear that there's a reason behind it, but I'll never know what it is.

"Please don't say anything," I beg Melissa. "Please."

TEXTILES AND FIBERS

I learned to crochet backward in Girl Scouts. We were earning our Textiles and Fibers badge. The week before, we'd cross-stitched a sampler with the Girl Scout Promise on it. That was okay because we all took turns, and I only used my left hand, and it was no big deal.

This week, we were crocheting a baby blanket for Children's Hospital, and we did not take turns, and we had to use both hands, and it was a big deal. Everyone else wrapped yarn around hook with one hand; pulled yarn through loops with the other. Bad Hand couldn't wrap yarn around hook. Bad Hand couldn't pull yarn through loops, either. Bad Hand couldn't do anything. "I hate this!"

"That's because you aren't good at it," said Andrea.

"It's because of Bad Hand! It's useless!"

"Your right hand is your wrong hand," said Andrea.

"I'm left-handed, duh." I'm extra left-handed and Andrea's extra idiotic.

"No, you're *wrong*-handed."

I hated Andrea most of the time, but especially right
then, and I jabbed her in the stomach with my crochet hook.
Not enough to really hurt her, but Andrea was a whiner,
and she moaned like she was dying. Sister Deb gave me a
look, like *Emily, stop. I know she's annoying, but* stop.

I stopped.

Andrea got a bunch of the younger girls to chant with
her: "Wrong-handed, wrong-handed."

Nobody made *them* stop. Maybe because I didn't
whine about it. What could I say? They were right: I've always been wrong-handed.

Still, if you ask me which is worse, poking someone
with a crochet hook or damaging her self-esteem by calling her wrong-handed, I've had enough Positive Action to
know what I'd answer.

But that's just me.

At a "fun for the whole family" church dinner. There is no such thing as "fun for the whole family" when you're a twelve-year-old girl.

REMBRANDT

The first boy I fell in love with didn't exist.

The whole thing starts in sixth-grade art class. It starts before the accident, before the Mounds bar, before I can put words to what's wrong with me.

Sixth grade is the first year we actually *have* an art class. Every Wednesday from two fifteen to two fifty-five, we go to Mrs. Stewart's room for art. Her students, the other sixth-grade class, go to our classroom for social studies.

I love art class. Art class has nothing to do with school art. School art is about following instructions and adding your own vision to a vision somebody else already had. In our regular class, we still do that, of course. In our regular class, we just finished spray-painting tin cans to look like pumpkins, and as soon as they dry, we will use stencils to draw on jack-o'-lantern faces.

But art class is about real art, and we are studying the Great Masters. When we file into the class, it's like I push the *pause* button on my sixth-grade life. My assigned seat is at the front of the classroom, and I drown out everything but the artists, everything but the art. Whatever's happened in my regular life doesn't matter: missing the ball when I was up to kick in PE, missing the punch line of Kacie's joke at recess, missing the point of Just Say No! assemblies and broom hockey and string art.

Only Johanna. Johanna sits in the back of the classroom, and I hate her being where I can't see her. I know how creepy and stalkerish that is to say. I know how much I sound like a jealous boyfriend, one of those crazy guys they end up discussing on afternoon talk shows.

But my friendship with Johanna is fragile, a Rumpelstiltskin deal that reserves the right to disappear at any time, for any reason. I've worked years for this friendship. So I worry: If I can't see her, she'll forget about me. She'll forget why we're friends. She'll only see the loser with the matted hair in the front row and think: *Psycho. So dense.*

Today, when we file into art class, there's a substitute teacher. During lunch, Mrs. Stewart's class told us their sub is chill so they're being cool to her. We do the same. We're not about to be less cool than Mrs. Stewart's class.

We get out our art notebooks, and the sub is cool, like they said. Her lips are deep red, like velvet, but it doesn't look fake. She's filling the board with stories about Rembrandt, and I am diligently copying them down. *BORN IN LEIDEN, HOLLAND, 1606. DID MOST OF HIS WORK IN AMSTERDAM. BAROQUE STYLE.*

The substitute teacher must not have gone to the same college as the regular teachers, though. They all write like a ruler, with big and small letters as appropriate. She uses all caps.

I don't even notice until I realize I'm doing it, too: copying her notes exactly, in all uppercase. *WELL-LIKED BECAUSE HE MADE PEOPLE LOOK GOOD IN PAINTINGS. THEN HIS WIFE DIED. WHEN HE STARTED PAINTING HOW HE FELT, EVERYONE REFUSED TO BUY HIS PORTRAITS.*

Something's off, so I double-check. Writing it was so natural, but now it looks like I'm reading something someone else wrote. And I've flipped some of my letters. It doesn't look wrong until I stare at it, hard, the way anything looks wrong if you stare at it too hard.

My *L*s turn backward. Same with my *B*s and *D*s. It's like reading my Disneyland logo shirt in the mirror. The look of it pleases me: tall, angular, slanted. I could write like this forever.

There's giggling behind me, giggling and whispers that make the back of my neck itch, so I know it's about me. I try to be sly, look over my shoulder like I'm stretching. Kacie's leaning over Johanna's desk, and they're laughing but not looking at me, and it's impossible to tell what they're actually laughing at.

I've been through enough therapy to know that sometimes it's all in my head.

But I've been through enough sixth grade to know that sometimes they're laughing at me.

When I press the *pause* button on my life, I am only kidding myself, because I'm not magic—the rest of sixth grade doesn't pause. I'm just playing pretend like a four-year-old, pretending I'm an art student studying in Paris, while everybody else is continuing with their real lives. They still get jokes and broom hockey and string art. I still don't.

I can push *pause* as many times as I want, but I will never be able to take a break from myself.

And this handwriting. It's not mine. I wish it were, but it's like any break I try to take from myself: temporary. My handwriting is careful and deliberate: capital letters where capital letters should be, lowercase the rest of the time. If left to their own devices, my words slope downward like a runaway toboggan. According to *Teen* magazine's article on handwriting analysis, this means I have a pessimistic outlook on life, which I have never doubted. My handwriting is *me* and it is not these slanted caps.

But still. These letters, these symbols, this hand: They belong to someone.

I just haven't found out who yet.

MOUNDS BAR

Johanna invites me to go shopping Monday afternoon the week after Thanksgiving, but she makes sure I know exactly where we stand. I walk across the street and down the block to her house to pick her up, and she says: "You weren't my first choice, you know." This seems unnecessary. Of course I wasn't her first choice. Johanna is my best friend, but I'm not her best friend. With Johanna, I've always taken whatever I can get.

We're going to the strip mall with the movie theater and the candy shop mysteriously named the Nut Factory and the Supercuts and the Payless ShoeSource. It's surrounded by busy streets, and I never thought of walking there until the first time Johanna invited me. Behind Johanna's house is a secret passage hidden by hedges. You push them aside, and magically you're back by the Dumpsters and service entrances and employees on their smoke break. It's the crème de la crème of shortcuts.

We are twelve years old, so we don't buy much when we go shopping. I've made it a point, though, to buy a Mounds bar on every excursion. I tried my first Mounds bar on a whim one day at the Nut Factory and was hooked. I like how Mounds bars come divided in half, so you know just which part is for now and which part is for later. I suck on chocolate and coconut and see how long I can make it last before it disintegrates. I like a good value.

I'm thinking maybe Mounds bars can become my thing, the way in The Baby-Sitters Club goody-gobbling Claudia has to have junk food and hippie-chick Dawn has to have health food and diabetic Stacey has to have sugar-free food. Maybe people will start thinking about me the same way, and it will become my trademark. Nobody will say: *Emily's that brainy loser.* They'll say: *Emily has to have Mounds bars.*

"So what's Erin doing tonight?" I ask, trying to sound like it doesn't bother me.

We start walking and Johanna looks at me, impressed that I put it together. But how stupid does she think I am? All she talks about these days is Erin, her super mature next-door neighbor who's in seventh grade.

I remember Erin from last year. She has a pointy nose and waist-length hair that she once wore in braids looped around her ears. She looked like Heidi, like she belonged in the Swiss Alps a hundred years ago, but no one made fun of her. She wasn't popular, but she wasn't the kind of girl you made fun of. I can see why Johanna wants her as a best friend.

"She has auditions for *West Side Story*. That's the junior high musical."

"Got it," I say. Johanna thinks I'm such a moron sometimes. It's times like these when I bring up Adrianna. "Adrianna was in *West Side Story* last year," I say. "She played Maria."

Adrianna's my friend from when I went to live with my grandmother for a few months in fourth grade. Adrianna is a year older than I am, with long black hair and piercing eyes. She's into drama and art, a rebel girl. She is as fictional as the day is long.

I used to walk home from school imagining the adventures we had together. We were in the school musical *The Sound of Music*. She was Liesl and I was Brigitta, because I was younger. She French-braided my hair and knew how not to pull too tight, and I'd go over to her house and eat licorice and rehearse lines, and we'd make fun of the dumb kids, who were all the kids except us.

And I'd walk home alone, remembering all these things that never happened, and it made the bad days not so bad, so by the time I got home, I wasn't crying anymore and I could forget what had happened at my real school in my real life.

This was before I had Johanna, of course. As much as I have ever had Johanna.

I don't think Johanna is listening about Adrianna. "It's so obvious Tyron likes Erin. Penelope says he's trying out for *West Side Story* just so he can drool over her." When she throws in names I don't know, it's always a bad sign. But I don't know what else to do—Adrianna was the only bright, shiny trinket in my bag of tricks.

I'm listening to Johanna talk about the church basketball game and which movie they saw at whose house, and I'm treading water, trying not to sink in people, places, and things she doesn't even want me to understand.

If I were not so heartsick-afraid of losing her, I'd call her on it. Instead, I see backward-slanted caps flash in front of my eyes. "I used to think Rembrandt liked Adrianna, but he told me he likes someone else."

Johanna stops short, right in front of the overgrown hedges. She's surprised I interrupted her. So am I. "Rembrandt?"

I nod. "You know, my best friend. Best *guy* friend, I mean."

"Your best guy friend." Johanna repeats it slowly, like the words are Japanese. I can't tell if it's because she doesn't believe me or just doesn't believe I could have a guy friend, but either way I'm more determined to make it real.

"Yeah." I say it like it doesn't matter. I pull back the scratchy hedges, duck my head, and snag my hair anyway. "He lives next door to my grandma. Haven't I ever mentioned him before? We used to play all the time. Now we just hang out. You know how it is."

For the first time, Johanna trails after me.

"I always thought he had a crush on Adrianna. But I

saw him last weekend, and when we were talking, he said something I think you'll want to know."

In reality, when I went to my grandma's last weekend, I sat on her wooden deck, next to the dryer vent where the hot, Grandma-scented air seeped into the November not-quite-cold. My two brothers played on the teeter-totter, and I watched them by myself.

But in the picture I show Johanna, I erase my brothers and add Rembrandt, a tall, dark-haired, slightly gawky but still cute fourteen-year-old who loves art and tennis and writes in backward caps.

"Why would *I* want to know?"

"Because." I pause before announcing it, the simple, perfect solution. "He doesn't like Adrianna. He likes you."

PURPLE SHOELACES

Rembrandt was the right move. Johanna's intrigued, excited, impressed—I can tell, even though she plays it nonchalant. "What do you mean, he likes me? He doesn't even know me."

"He knows enough. I talk about you all the time. And I showed him that picture of us from when we were lunch servers."

All the fifth and sixth graders take turns serving lunch. You don't get a choice. Most kids like to be lunch servers because you get to miss class and you don't have to make up the work, plus you get seconds of dessert. But I don't like school desserts (except for raspberry Cutie Pies, which are hardly ever on the menu). And the serving itself was, as expected, a disaster.

I was at the salad station. Instead of using tongs, I had

to use two plastic-gloved hands to scoop salad onto the front square section of the lunch tray. Only, my right hand is my wrong hand, and about three scoopfuls into the day, Bad Hand started shaking and not behaving, like it always does. I slowed down so the shaking wouldn't make the salad spill into the front rectangle section of the tray, where the mashed potatoes with beef and gravy were supposed to go, because when that happened, kids complained. Except slowing down backed up the line and kids complained even more, and the lunch ladies wondered what was going on, and I tried not to cry, so of course I *did* cry.

It was not a good day. But the Polaroid picture Mrs. Manwaring took right before lunch is the only full-color proof I have of Johanna and me. We stood side by side, in disposable aprons that smelled like a nursing home, and matching ponytails, tight so we didn't have to wear hairnets. We didn't look like real best friends with arms around each other and peace signs and crossed-eyes and stuck-out tongues. But we looked close.

"You showed him a picture of me serving lunch?"

I shrug and play it off as funny, not pathetic. "What? It was all I had. And anyway, he thought it was cute." I say it confident, because I don't know so many things, but when it comes to Rembrandt, I know about love. "So he wrote you a letter."

We go into Payless. We go into every store when we go shopping.

"Whatever you do," I say to Johanna, while the chiming bells announce our entrance into the store, "don't make fun of Rembrandt's name. He thinks it's *so* immature."

"No duh, I wouldn't do that," says Johanna, and I breathe a sigh of relief, because I've cleared the first hurdle: getting her to buy into the name Rembrandt.

"That's what I told him. I said, 'No worries; Johanna's not like that. Just write to her and see what happens.' I was going to bring the letter tonight, but I didn't have anywhere to put it."

"So tomorrow." Johanna says it casual.

"Tomorrow."

We never look at shoes we might actually want to buy. We make fun of the little-kid sneakers with Mario and Luigi on the side, and we pick out the ugliest pairs in the whole store and decide which teacher would wear them. Now that it is winter and almost snow, the boots are out, and Johanna says, "Ooh, hooker boots!"

"What?" I can't help giggling like a stereotypical twelve-year-old girl. I don't do it often and it feels good. "What are hooker boots?" I've never heard anyone use the term *hooker*, but I know what it means. Sometimes you just know.

"See?" Johanna grabs a pair of boots: shiny black leather, tall enough that they're past her knees, although I don't know how high they'd come on a prostitute. Stiletto heel. "These are the kind of boots hookers wear. Didn't you know that?"

"Uh, no, I did not know that." I roll my eyes. "Why would I know that?" As far as I know, there are no prostitutes in Midvalley. At least not the kind who wear hooker boots.

"Didn't you see them before? Where you used to live?"

She means Driftwood Park. I saw a lot of things in Driftwood Park. Hooker boots were not among them. I don't want to talk about what I saw in Driftwood Park.

"Look! These are way better," I say. On a clear shelf sticking out of the wall are way-better boots. Not ironically way-better, either. The boots are soft black suede waffle-stompers with purple shoelaces. "They're Punky Brewster boots!"

Punky Brewster is the free-spirited, mismatching preteen in the sitcom *Punky Brewster.* I loved that show—tuned in every week, even during the summer when all the episodes were reruns I'd already seen. It went off the air two seasons back, and TV hasn't been worth watching since.

"Is that supposed to be a good thing?" Johanna asks, turning a hooker boot over in her hand like a globe on an axis.

"It is most definitely a good thing. These boots are awesome." I'm feeling giddy, and it is all because of Rembrandt. Rembrandt would love these boots as much as I do. "I'm coming back here tomorrow, and I'm buying these boots."

And I do. I buy the boots with the purple shoelaces.

REMBRANDT'S FIRST LETTER

DEAR JOHANNA,
SO IF YOU ARE READING THIS, IT MEANS EM
TALKED TO YOU ABOUT ME AND GAVE YOU THIS
AND YOU ARE (HOPEFULLY) STILL READING IT. I
KNOW IT'S KIND OF WEIRD TO GET A LETTER FROM
A GUY YOU'VE NEVER MET . . . BUT JUST THINK OF
IT THIS WAY: IT'S KIND OF WEIRD TO WRITE TO A
GIRL YOU'VE NEVER MET! BUT EM TOLD ME ABOUT
YOU AND YOU SOUND COOL, SO I THOUGHT I'D
JUST WRITE AND SEE WHAT HAPPENS.

ANYWAY, MY NAME IS REMBRANDT BECAUSE
MY PARENTS ARE ARTIST FREAKS, BUT THAT'S
COOL BECAUSE I AM, TOO. MY FAVORITE THINGS
RIGHT NOW ARE CHARCOAL DRAWING AND
PHOTOGRAPHY. I ALSO LIKE TENNIS. WHAT ARE
YOU INTO? WHAT KIND OF MUSIC DO YOU LIKE?
RIGHT NOW MY FAVORITE SONGS ARE ALL U2.

MY PARENTS ARE ACTUALLY PRETTY COOL AND
KIND OF HIPPIE, BUT THEY ARE STRANGELY
OVERPROTECTIVE SOMETIMES, SO I THINK THEY'D
FREAK OUT IF I STARTED GETTING MAIL FROM A
GIRL. SO IF YOU WANT TO WRITE BACK, JUST GIVE
THE LETTER TO EM AND SHE CAN GET IT TO ME.
WE SEE EACH OTHER PRETTY OFTEN.

I HOPE YOU DO WRITE BACK AND TELL ME ABOUT
YOURSELF. AND IF YOU HAVE QUESTIONS ABOUT
ME YOU CAN ASK.

PEACE.

REMBRANDT

P.S. I HOPE YOU CAN READ THIS. SOMETIMES MY
LETTERS TURN BACKWARD AS YOU'VE PROBABLY
NOTICED. A TEACHER CALLED IT "ILLEGIBLE"
ONCE, AND I GOT MARKED DOWN ON MY
ASSIGNMENT AND IT SUCKED. NOT THE GRADE
PART (WHO CARES?) BUT THAT SHE'D DO IT
BECAUSE OF MY HANDWRITING.

P.P.S. I READ THIS ART BOOK ABOUT DA VINCI AND
HE WROTE IN BACKWARD LETTERS SOMETIMES, SO
I PERSONALLY DON'T SEE ANYTHING WRONG WITH
IT. I THINK IT'S BECAUSE DA VINCI AND I ARE BOTH
LEFT-HANDED. AND EM. SO SCREW "ILLEGIBLE."

P.P.P.S. EM SAYS YOU WON'T BELIEVE THIS, BUT YOU
REALLY DO LOOK PRETTY HOT IN THAT PICTURE.

P.P.P.P.S. YOU WILL NEVER BE ABLE TO WRITE AS
MANY P.S.'S AS ME. I AM THE P.S. CHAMPION!!

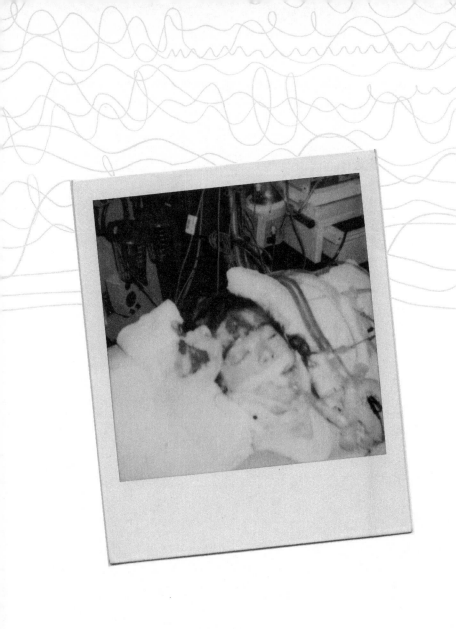

"Some people are safe, some people aren't. I'm not."

WAKING UP

I am not surprised to be here.

That's the first thought I have when I wake up in ICU. *I knew this day was coming.*

When something bad happens to you early on, you're not surprised when bad things keep happening. It's what you're used to. It's one of the rules you make up for life because you don't know otherwise yet: *Some people are safe, some people aren't. I'm not.* I made up that rule when I was five years old. That's why now, at twelve years old, I realize it so easily.

My parents are standing over me, in washed-out colors with weak smiles. If they're standing over me, it means they're safe. And if they're together, it means they didn't have to split up to visit anyone else. So the other kids are safe.

I am the only one who isn't safe.

I can tell immediately that I'm in a hospital—it's the little, subtle things. First off, we're in a room that isn't actually a room. It's what I imagine the inside of a circus tent to look like. There's the pale pink barf bucket at my side. There are sterile white blankets. There's a heart-rate monitor next to me. There's noise from an intercom.

All things I associate with hospitals, although I've never stayed in one for any length of time before. I've known it was coming, though. It feels like forever that I've known this day was coming.

Blinking hurts, and it takes much longer than it usually does. One eye isn't opening. Why isn't one eye opening? My immediate reaction is to touch it—grab my eyelid and *make* it open—but my arm moves slow and clunky. That's not right. I start to say *This isn't right*, and when I can't say *This isn't right*, that's when I know this really isn't right.

Because I expected to be able to talk, but no. It's like an apple core is stuck in my throat. And I expected to be able to use my hands, but no, there are a bunch of tubes and wires sticking out everywhere, and my wrists are strapped to boards. And I expected to be able to blink, but no. It's now painfully obvious that one eye is swollen shut.

"You were in a car accident," Mom says. "You and Johanna went shopping. You got hit by a car crossing the street on the way home."

I don't have to ask if Johanna is okay. She doesn't have to cross the street when we go shopping. Only I cross the street. *Try* to cross the street.

"We're at Children's Hospital now." Mom's still talking, but I'm a half beat behind. "They're taking good care of you. They've already started fixing you up. Do you want to see?"

She holds up a hand mirror, already at her side. It's been expected, that I would wake up and need to see the damage. She adjusts it so I can take in the whole picture.

All I can think about is The Baby-Sitter's Club #60, *Mary Anne's Makeover*, which I just finished last week. Mary Anne is the mousy club member who looks like a little girl still, and she used to have to wear clothes her dad picked out and keep her hair in pigtails. But by the end of book #4, she's choosing her own outfits and letting her hair down, and a mere fifty-six volumes later, she's getting an entire new wardrobe complete with salon haircut and department-store makeup. And someone holds a mirror to her face, and she looks into it and she's beautiful, and she is not a little girl anymore.

But when my mother holds a mirror to my face and I look into it, I wish I didn't. I gasp. Even when I think I know what's coming, I gasp. I'm usually pale, but this is paler than pale. My freckles stand out like chocolate stains on a white cloth napkin. My left eye is all the shades of blue and purple and indigo of the pastels in my neglected art set. My lips are chapped and translucent.

But it's my forehead. That's where they've fixed me up. It's bad, but it's the kind of bad you look at and know it has been much worse. My bangs are clipped back, and right between my eyes, just above my nose, there it is: an upside-down Y that looks like it's about to drip blood. I know it isn't. It was once a gash, but now it's a wound. Soon it will be a scar.

And I will always, forever, see that face when I look in the mirror.

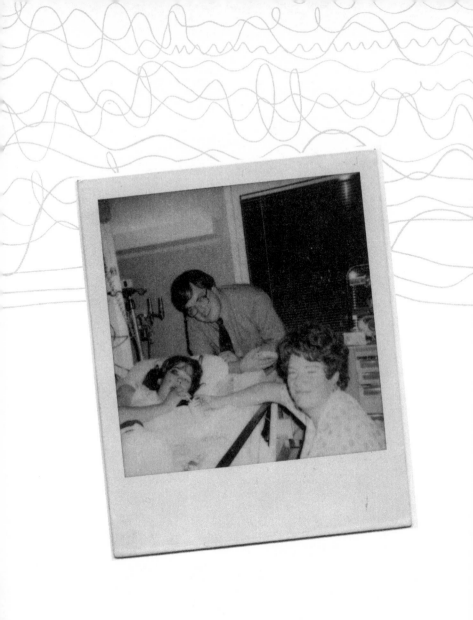

"My parents are standing over me, in washed-out colors
with weak smiles."

THE NEXT TIME I WAKE UP

When I wake up again, I am aware time has passed, but I don't know how much time. It could be 7:00 a.m. or 7:00 p.m.; I have no idea which. I hate that feeling, the disorientation of not knowing if it's morning or night or the next day.

My parents are still here. They ask me if I want something to drink. They say the respirator is gone now, but my throat is still as sore as it was before. They say the hospital has all kinds of drinks—every kind of juice you can imagine, and soda pop.

"My braces," I say, my voice hoarse. The first words I speak after the accident are to remind my mom and dad I'm not supposed to drink juice or soda, not with braces. My orthodontist told me so. I play by the rules.

They nod solemnly. I think they forgot about my braces. My mom goes to get me some water.

Dad says, "Emily, do you know what a brain tumor is?"

Yes. I do know what a brain tumor is. I'm relieved that as sick as I am, I still have the smart-girl recall that's become my personal trademark. I may be a loser, but I'm a smart loser, with a mind like a steel trap. I remember everything.

I read a book about a girl with a brain tumor. This mass of craziness in her head keeps getting bigger and bigger, and it's her dying wish to go to Disney World, so her sister sneaks her out of the hospital to make her dream come true. When you have an out-of-control mass of craziness in your head, the end is inevitable.

I wonder if a different girl, a girl lying on the other side of the blue circus-tent curtain, has a brain tumor.

A brain tumor is the kind of thing I always thought I'd have. A real out-of-control mass of craziness in my head to explain the out-of-control craziness I've always *felt* in my head. Something we would discover and say, "Ah, so this explains it." And I would lie in a hospital bed very much like this one, and I would not look like a boxer in a title fight; I would look like an elegant Victorian princess.

They'd all line up to see me as I lay with my arms folded across my chest, holding a red rose, midbloom. "I'm sorry," they'd say. "I didn't realize there was an out-of-control mass of craziness in your head. No one who is dying deserves to be treated the way I treated you." Lots of people would be saying that. The kids from the neighborhood. The kids from school. My sister. My parents. They would all beg my forgiveness, which I would graciously bestow with my parting breath, and then I would be taken from this earth, never again to deal with the pain and suffering I had endured for so long.

But I don't have a brain tumor. I have a car accident. So I tell my father: "It's something people get in their head and then they die."

And he pauses before he says it. "Sometimes people die. But they don't think you will."

It doesn't make sense. I don't have a brain tumor. I have a car accident. I'm not a Victorian princess; I'm a beat-up twelve-year-old with braces.

It doesn't make sense, but then it does, and then it hurts to keep my eye open, so I close it and my last thought is, *I have a brain tumor* and *I have a car accident.*

THE MIRACLE

It's stupid to play What If: *What if Johanna had gone shopping with Erin that night instead of me? What if I'd stayed home and helped my mom with dinner? What if I'd headed home ten seconds sooner?*

It's a stupid game because I know the accident would have happened no matter what. I know the accident was a blessing, a miracle. I've heard it a thousand times already—I'm the Thank-God-She-Got-Hit-By-A-Car Girl.

The slow-growing astrocytoma camping out in my cerebellum was getting bigger every day, winding around the brain stem, encroaching on the ventricle that let cerebrospinal fluid keep me alive. The tumor would have killed me, so I needed it gone, and it's gone now.

But it wouldn't be. Not if a car hadn't hit me on a December night. Not if I hadn't been airlifted to a hospital that would give me a CT scan to assess injuries and note the grapefruit-size mass at the base of my skull.

Now the only evidence that I ever had a brain tumor is the railroad-track incision along the right side of my head. And the clumps of hair they had to shave for surgery. They saved it all for me, in a clear plastic bag labeled SPECIMEN TRANSPORT. The specimen is a whole lot of brown hair.

Still, everyone comments on how much hair I have left—my parents, the plastic surgeon who works on my forehead, the child life specialist who comes by once "just to talk." They say, "You look pretty good for having just had brain surgery" or "Most patients don't leave brain surgery with a head full of hair." They say it with look-on-the-bright-side, cheer-you-up smiles. And I know it cheers them up.

It's not like I don't believe it's a miracle. I know everybody's right. I know I'm lucky.

But the right side of my head feels too light now, and too cold, and whenever the right side of my body shakes, I can't stop it. My fingers clatter against the board Bad Hand is taped to, and it strikes me that my woozy-head has only gotten stronger.

Sometimes I think I might have died in the accident, and now my body is haunted. Sometimes I feel like this otherworldly spirit has taken over, and I have to let it do its thing before I can move on in my journey to leave Earth and meet God. I haven't heard or felt God the whole time I've been in the hospital, even though if everyone else is to be believed, He's to thank that I'm in here.

Sometimes it's hard to trust the miracle. Because that's the funny thing about me and good luck. My good luck is so rarely lucky.

C-H-R-I-S-T-I-E

This time I wake up alone. It's the first time at the hospital that I've woken up and my parents haven't been here. They told me it might happen, but it never has, not until now. I don't miss them. I'm glad they're finally back home. But I wish they were here to tell me what time it is.

A lady with permed hair comes in while I'm blinking the sleep from my good eye. Bad Eye is doing better, but blinking's a ways off. The lady says her name is Christie and she's the night nurse and not to worry. She must think I'm one of those kids who worry when their mom and dad aren't right there next to them, but I'm fine alone. I've been alone all my life.

"I'm just going to change your lines real quick," she says.

I don't know what lines are, but it does not occur to

me to ask this. It occurs to me to ask: "How do you spell your name?" Because, you know, first things first. When people have a name with various spellings, I like to know immediately how they spell it, so I'm not seeing it wrong in my mind when I say it. She spells it for me, and I see the letters appear in front of my eyes and I like it and I tell her so and she says thank you.

C-H-R-I-S-T-I-E. I know she is not my first nurse—I must have had nurses up to this point; I just haven't met them. I know she will not be my last nurse. I want to remember her anyway.

She says, "You've had a pretty rough go of it these last couple of days. And with the brain tumor you didn't even know about, growing so big, causing you headaches and what-all else, well . . . you've probably had a pretty rough go of it for a while now."

Rough go is a phrase I've never heard used before in real life, but I'm inclined to agree with her.

"Don't worry. The doctors, they fixed you up. We'll take good care of you."

The pillow used to prop me up has slid down my back, but because my hands are taped to lines, I can't do anything to fix it. I don't want to ask Christie while she's changing my lines, but the pillow makes me jut forward so I look pregnant.

"We'll take good care of you," she says again, finishing up. She sees my pillow and tells me to lean forward. She fluffs the pillow and tucks it behind my neck. "Everything will be okay now, Emily. Now you can heal. Now you can get better."

I like Christie. Love her, maybe. She's young and kind, and even just the sound of her voice convinces me she'd lie down in traffic if it meant protecting a kid. She means it when she says, "Now you can get better." She means it as a promise, not a threat.

Doctors don't know how long the tumor was nesting in my brain, but they know it was a very long time, maybe since I was born, maybe even before that. Now we know that so much of what I thought was me was really the tumor.

They say it's probably because of the tumor that I've spent my life sick and clumsy and weak on my right side. Probably because of the tumor that I'm extra left-handed. Probably because of the tumor that I've never been the kind of girl who responded to treatment. Therapy didn't work on me. Glasses didn't work on me. Do I really believe surgery worked on me?

Because the tumor is gone now, and still, I have a woozy-head. Still, I think I might be haunted. Still, I wonder stupid things, like how my nurse spells her name.

I'm lucky, having something real wrong with me. The tumor gave me an excuse for being backward, an excuse for being the weird girl. Now that excuse is gone. Now it's time to heal. Now I can get better.

Only what if I can't?

DAMIEN'S DAD

I was eating a Mounds bar.

I'm out of ICU now, on the Rehabilitation floor. Now I have a real room with walls and a TV and a window. I can have visitors here, and they're mostly my mom and dad's friends, or older ladies from church. They bring teddy bears or Christmas cookies with sprinkles, and they talk about where they were that night, how they found out, and every story is different, but they all share one sameness.

They know that when I got hit, I was eating a Mounds bar.

People were at the scene, of course. People I barely know, who now feel we are intimately connected because they've seen me ghost-skinned and bleeding. But they're the same to me as they were before, unfamiliar names with blurry faces attached.

Lonny Bitner's mom was there. She had been a nurse in a long-ago life. My mom told me. She said Lonny Bitner's mom moved my head back so I wouldn't choke on blood. Lonny used to be in our ward, and I sat behind him in Primary. The Primary Presidency always had to threaten to get Lonny's mom if he didn't behave, and once they actually did it, and she sat next to him with her arms folded and her lips tight all during Singing Time, and that was all I knew about Lonny's mom.

Now I know she was there when it happened.

And Damien's dad. Damien's dad was there when it happened.

They called him Mr. Topps when they told me. As soon as I could think to ask anything, I asked my parents: "Does anyone know who hit me? Was it a hit-and-run?" It seemed like it should be a hit-and-run, like no one would have bothered stopping for a girl like me on an only-sort-of busy street.

It wasn't a hit-and-run. It was kind of worse; because they told me the driver's name was Patrick Topps. I said I knew a Damien Topps at school and the driver was probably his teenage brother. It seemed like it should have been a teenage driver, inexperienced behind the wheel, who would hit a girl like me on an only-sort-of-busy street.

It wasn't a teenage driver. It was kind of worse, because they told me it was his father. A normal, middle-aged driver. The father of a popular boy. Hitting an unpopular girl like me. On an only-sort-of-busy street.

Damien is in my grade, but he has never, not in six

years, been in my class. Everyone in sixth grade knows Damien except me. Damien is the real-life equivalent of *Beverly Hills, 90210,* the TV show that everybody else watches and talks about, but I can't join in.

Every single boy in sixth grade says Damien's a sports superstar, and I assume it's true because I don't know who's good at sports. Every single girl in sixth grade says Damien's cute, and I assume it's true because I don't know who's cute. Damien doesn't look cute to me; he looks normal.

What will he look like now?

LAUNDRY LIST

The Mounds bar is one of the laundry list of items that make up what I know about the accident. The Mounds bar. My purple shoelaces. My glasses. My glasses survived the accident without a scratch. Big, plastic tortoiseshell frames completely intact. While a half inch above them, my forehead was crushed.

My purple shoelaces. They survived. They were how my mother recognized me. That night, she looked out the kitchen window and saw traffic backing up and realized I wasn't home yet. She opened the front door and saw ambulance lights in the distance, and she ran to them, ran out into the street, her panic surpassing fear. Was this her daughter, this girl with an oxygen mask and hair pulled back, covered in blood? This girl, bare from the waist up with a blanket wrapped around her chest, was this *her* girl?

She didn't know—at that point, not even my indestructible glasses were on.

All she remembered was the time I'd come home two weeks earlier, asking for the black boots with the purple shoelaces. So she asked a paramedic if the girl's shoelaces were purple, and he said yes.

And the Mounds bar. Everyone knows the Mounds bar—the part I hadn't eaten yet, anyway—survived the accident. *Emily has to have Mounds bars.*

So the Mounds bar lasted, and the glasses lasted, and the shoelaces lasted. The items lasted, but the memory didn't. I think of that night and I can't remember it, and I think of the night before it, and I can't remember it.

My mom told me about the week after Thanksgiving, about finding the boots with the purple shoelaces, and it sounds like something that might have happened to me, but I can't see a picture of it. What is the last night I can see a picture of?

Columbus Day. I see a picture of Columbus Day night. We'd rehearsed *Chris Crossed*, the sixth-grade musical, for weeks. I delivered backstory by playing Student #4, a role made more difficult because we couldn't dress like regular students. I wore a black skirt and white shirt, and the teachers made bows that each of us had to wear around our neck, and I couldn't tie mine, and Johanna sighed and said "Let me do it," and I was so relieved, even though I knew I shouldn't have been. I knew she wasn't just pretending to be annoyed—she was actually annoyed. She wanted a best friend who could tie her own bow and knew who Damien

Topps was and didn't hit someone when she got mad like a kindergartner would.

And since I have been in the hospital, I have not heard from Johanna, not a card or a visit or a call, even though I have my own phone now, in this room with the window and the walls. And the pictures I see in my mind aren't dates anymore, or events; they are just memories of Johanna and me, and I get it.

I get that Johanna and me, we were over long before the Mounds bar.

Columbus Day school play.

A BLANK BOOK
AND A PINK PEN

"You're getting a visitor this afternoon," Mom says. "A special one."

I have my hospital bed raised so I can sit up, and the bedside table has been wheeled over me so I can write. The menu they've given me has REGULAR DIET across the top in big letters. Now that I can eat normal food, I'm supposed to circle what I want for dinner: oven-baked chicken, meat loaf, baked potato with sour cream, carrots, Waldorf salad, tossed salad, spice cake. It all sounds good. I've been wondering how many things I can circle.

Only now I'm wondering about my surprise visitor. Johanna? No, stop hoping it's Johanna. "Who is it?"

Mom just shakes her head and smiles.

"Okay, well then, how do I look?"

"You could probably use some lip balm?" Mom says

hopefully. She knows I hate wearing it. It feels thick and slick, and the right side of my face tingles in a numb way the other side doesn't. I try hard not to notice the numbness, but when there's stuff on my lips, I notice the numbness. I nod, though. I know my lips are peeling, that sometimes there's blood.

Mom got me a Pina Colada Lip Smacker because that's my favorite kind of Slurpee. She's been so nice to me since I've been here. I wonder if she was nice to me before the accident, too—if it started during those weeks I can't remember.

There's a knock at the door. I know it can't be my nurse Jerry; he never knocks. It's unsettling. He's kind of old and looks like Pee-wee Herman, and he jokes with me all the time like we're friends. We aren't.

"That's probably her," my mom says. Then louder: "Come in!"

Johanna? No, stop hoping it's Johanna.

"Hello?" she says, cracking open the door and poking her face in.

My heart jumps to my throat and explodes there.

It's not Johanna. It's better than Johanna, because it's someone I never expected would come, and now she's here. Miss Beck.

She opens the door the rest of the way. I've never seen her wear jeans before today, and she's paired them with a Brigham Young University sweatshirt, the oversized letters B, Y, and U stitched in shiny blue satin. It's another piece of her wardrobe I've never seen. She looks like a different person, not my teacher.

I've always liked my teachers, but Miss Beck is different.

When other teachers got mad at me, I was embarrassed and sick inside, and it bothered me because they were grown-ups and I wanted to please them, and I'd let them down. I want to please Miss Beck, too, maybe even more than I've wanted to please the others, but when she's upset with me, it doesn't feel like being scolded. It feels personal, like hearing your best friend talk about you behind your back, like fighting words, like a broken heart.

"Come, sit down." Mom gets up from the blue armchair, the only comfortable place to sit in the room. "I'm going to get something to eat from the cafeteria."

Miss Beck smiles at her and sits down. "I want to ask how you're feeling," she says, "but it seems like a dumb question, given the situation."

"I'm okay!" I say, sitting up higher. "I'm so much better now. That's why I'm on this floor. I have my own TV and phone and everything. It's more than I had at home!" I smile so she will, and she does, but it's not the kind of smile I was hoping for. There's still some sadness in it.

"You're strong," she says.

I shrug.

"You are," she says.

Miss Beck has sent me letters since I've been here. She writes in perfect cursive that slants the right way and has no mistakes, no cross-outs or scribbles or letters turned into other letters. She tells me not to worry about school, that the projects they're finishing up in class don't matter, because it's the holidays and vacation will start soon. She tells me not to think I'm missing anything important.

Looking at her, I think she knows, like I do, that I *am* missing something important. Every report on *The Westing Game* that I don't get to give takes me even farther away from the kids I was so far apart from at the start.

Now you can get better. But what if I can't?

"I got you something." Miss Beck pulls out her teacher bag: quilted, with a design of two cats napping on a stack of books. I know that bag. That bag comforts me. "Here," she says, and she sits at the foot of my bed and hands me a shiny package.

I tear it open, forgetting to be careful so I can save the wrapping paper. It's a blank book covered in soft, floral fabric, and a fountain pen, ink the same color as the tiny roses on the book's cover. It's exquisite. "Thank you."

She smiles. "What else would I give a writer?" She says *writer*. She does not say *someone who likes to write*. "I know you'll have feelings and thoughts and story ideas from this experience. I hope these will help you put them down." She gives me a faux-stern look. "As soon as you're feeling well enough."

I want to prove to her I'm well enough already, show her my pencil and the menu and how I've been circling. But I don't need to impress her, so I just say it again. "Thank you."

—

The blank book from Miss Beck is the first thing that makes me realize that right now, right this minute, I am living my Before and After. That every day up to "this experience" was Before, and every day since, every day for the rest of my life, will be After.

I wonder if there will ever be a day when I don't think about it. If there will ever be a future for me that includes a day when my hair grows back thick and full over my incision, so I won't think about the tumor. Or if, after weeks of rubbing vitamin E oil over my forehead like Dr. Lucero told me to, my scar becomes so light that it blends in with my freckles and nobody asks about it and I don't think about the accident.

I can't imagine that day happening. I can't imagine the bristles not catching on the jagged, raised bump down the right side of my scalp each time I brush my hair. I can't imagine not looking in the mirror and seeing the scar and knowing that, no matter how faint it is, it's still a reminder of what made me feel a hundred years old when I was supposed to be a child.

MAUDE

My dad crushes Maude when I fall asleep.

Dad will go on streaks of playing one game at a time until he tires of it. For the last few months, it's been *Monopoly* on Game Boy. There are a bunch of computerized competitors, and he used to play against all of them. Since I've been in the hospital, he only plays against Maude, the toughest one.

"Hey," I say when my eyes flutter open and I see him in the blue chair at my bedside. "Crushing Maude?"

And he says yes, and he plays, and we listen for the hospitality cart to roll by. Sometimes it has jelly doughnuts, and when it does, he gets a raspberry one.

REMBRANDT'S VISIT

Rembrandt's the kind of guy who'd visit his friend in the hospital every day if he could. But he lives by my grandma, far from this hospital, so he only visits me once.

It's late on a day my parents left early, and I'm glad because they don't know about Rembrandt. Rembrandt is my friend and my friend alone. "Hey," he says when he sees me. "Nice crib."

I laugh because Rembrandt's this wannabe gangsta, fair-haired and blue-eyed, from a "hood" where everybody else is fair-haired and blue-eyed, too. "'Sup?" I put my hand out for a fist bump.

His hand is cold and he knows it, because he says: "Sorry. It's frigid out there, yo. I took the bus up here and it dropped me off, like, a block away."

I press my lips together and try to make it subtle. I

put on Pina Colada Lip Smacker right before he got here. "Thanks for making the trip."

He nods, like of course he'd make the trip, no question. Then he swings the blue chair around and sits on it backward. "That's quite the collection you've got there," he says, pointing to the row of stuffed bears lining the windowsill.

"Everyone sends bears." I think because the accident happened at Christmastime. I have white bears with Santa hats, white bears holding presents, white bears wearing scarves. There are other bears, too, of the more traditional teddy variety: light brown with purple bows, dark brown with pink bows, medium brown with big noses.

I don't think of—have never thought of—myself as a stuffed-animal person, but that's what everyone gives me. I guess they can't think of what else to do.

"Well, I did not bring you a bear," Rembrandt says, and unzips his JanSport backpack. "I did, however, bring M&M'S, a book of crossword puzzles, and a buttload of Laffy Taffy."

"Buttload?" I repeat, raising my eyebrows.

"Shut up," he says. "I was thinking the jokes would make you laugh."

There's a split-second stillness charged with air left over from what he said. It's maybe cheesy, maybe pathetic, but I feel it like a punch in the heart. He was thinking the jokes would make me laugh. He thought of me.

It's clear he wants me to say something, make this energetic stillness go away. "Thanks. You're the best." I give him a thumbs-up. It looks stupid.

He rolls his eyes. "So are we, like, confined to this room, or can you show me around?"

"I think that can be arranged," I say. "As long as you don't mind helping me push this thing around." I have a lumbar drain in, a tube coming out of my spine that's connected to a bunch of machinery that I have to wheel alongside me when I go anywhere, which is not often, because I have to wheel this thing, and there aren't that many places to go in a hospital anyway.

Rembrandt checks out my machinery and helps me out of bed. "Hey, sweet kicks."

I'm wearing thick socks with white rubbery treads on the bottom that they give to all the patients. "Shut up," I say, but he knows I want him to keep talking.

Only he doesn't, because we have to be kind of quiet and sly when we sneak out, because I don't know if I'm actually allowed to leave my room without an adult around. Rembrandt is the only friend who's come to visit me without my mom bringing them here.

"The physical therapy gym is on this floor," I tell him as we roll along. "I'll be going back there as soon as I get rid of this thing." I motion to the drain, but I have to be careful not to pull it out of my spine because the whole thing is so delicate. I pulled the drain out by accident once, and my nurse couldn't fix it and got annoyed, and I hated seeing that look on her face, like I was a bad patient.

"I would love to see you in a physical therapy gym." The idea of it cracks Rembrandt up, and I have to shush him. Even though watching me in a physical therapy gym *is* kind of funny—I mean, when it's not overwhelmingly sad.

I don't take him in the playroom; we go past it instead because I don't want us to get caught. There are a bunch of games in there, board games like Sorry! and arcade games like *Donkey Kong,* but there's always someone on staff there, and that's the last thing we need. So I take Rembrandt to the map at the stairwell and look for the location of a room I heard Mom mention once but where I've never been.

We take the elevator to the third floor and only walk a little before we see it: a stained-glass window about the size of a movie poster, lit up like a coming-attractions case at a theater. The colors shimmer: blues and reds with streaks of gold.

Rembrandt takes in a breath. "Wow. I was not expecting this."

"From what I've heard, there's a meditation room behind the window, this quiet place to sit and . . . I don't know, think? Want to look inside?" And he nods before I even finish the question.

The meditation room is breathtaking. The far wall is one giant window, making this place look like a cathedral, not a hospital. A table has copies of the Bible and prayer books spread across it. Plush couches are on either side, and Rembrandt helps me sink into one of them.

How long has it been since I sat on a couch? Reclined on furniture like a normal person? This is the perfect place to feel like a normal person. This is the perfect place to feel like a normal person with Rembrandt.

Rembrandt's going to sit next to me, but he sees something first. "Yo, Em, check it." He flips a switch and the stained-glass enclave darkens.

The window is transformed into a piece of art. Now I see angels emerge in the picture—angels playing mini harps. I'm overwhelmed with this feeling of peace I haven't felt in so long. Maybe ever. Here, I'm at one with God and Rembrandt, shielded by stained glass and cushy upholstery.

He flips another switch. The room goes completely dark.

The window is even more astonishing now, surrounded by blackness. It seems to be suspended in space. "Amazing," I say.

"Amazing," he agrees. I feel him lower his body next to mine and sit down.

I see his face only shadowed in the room, *feel* his handsome more than see it, and there is no mistaking how much I want to kiss him with my Pina Colada lips and have him all to myself. I think I might be in love with Rembrandt.

But I can't have him. In that way, that most important way, he belongs to Johanna and Johanna alone.

Still, that day with Rembrandt. What a beautiful, beautiful day.

I wish it had been real.

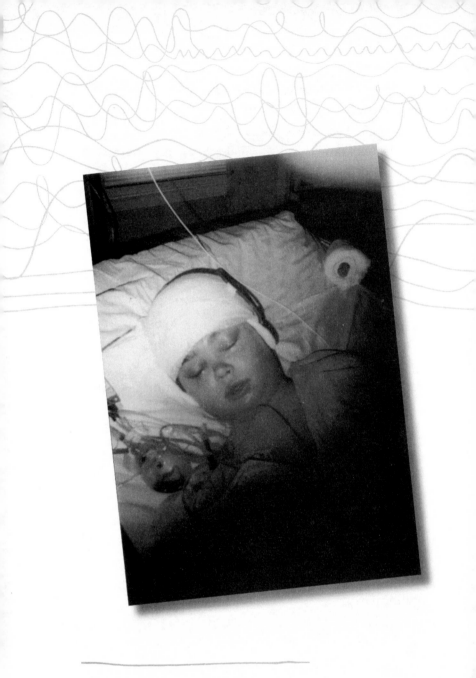

After the craniotomy. Is this hell?

DRINKING THE KOOL-AID

You know when you think things can't get worse and then they do?

Like, say maybe you're in the hospital because you got hit by a car and then—surprise!—it turns out you have a brain tumor, too? Well, say that happens to you and you think you're getting better. And things aren't great. But you think you're at the bottom, that all you can do is go up. Slowly. Painfully slowly. But still, up. Only with everyone spewing on about how lucky you are, you've forgotten your number one rule for life: You don't *go* up.

We've been talking about mucus a lot lately, the nurses and I.

Mucus is just one of the gross bodily things in a hospital that aren't cool-gross, i.e., blood and guts, but just gross-gross. In the weeks that I've been here, I've discovered many such bodily things.

Like, once I moved into my room, they took my catheter out and I started going to the bathroom again. The toilets are weird here, and sitting on one feels funny, like it's a booster seat. There's this plastic shelf under the lid and above the bowl that collects your pee, and after I go, I have to tell my nurses, and they go check it, and I have no idea what that involves, but *eww*.

The worst was when my Pee-wee Herman nurse, Jerry, came in with his clipboard and told me I hadn't pooped in four days and that was too long, so I had to go right away. I told him I didn't need to go. He said he'd find something to *make* me need to go. I didn't want something to make me need to go, and I wished so, so hard that he would go away and stop asking me about how often I pooped, and *eww*.

So anyway, mucus.

Apparently the stuff coming out of my nose that I assumed was regular run-of-the-mill snot is maybe not snot. It's clear and watery, and although mucus is tricky and can appear clear and watery, there's something called spinal fluid that's *always* clear and watery. The stuff coming out of my nose might be that.

If it is, it's because there's a crack in one of the bones in my forehead and they need to seal it up, and that means surgery. That means slicing my head open and peeling my face down and finding the broken bone and fixing it. It's one of the bodily things in a hospital that are cool-gross, I guess. But it makes me wish so, so hard for snot.

The doctors come by on their morning rounds. "This is not snot," they say. And I cry so hard that you can't tell the tears from the snot from the spinal fluid.

They make me sit in the waiting room like a normal person. My mom sits with me.

She's writing something in her planner, a short, fat, three-ringed notebook with a burgundy cover. She takes it everywhere. I flip through a *Family Circle* from December, and wonder what other moms read about last month while my mom was sitting with me in the hospital, writing lists in her planner about who to give thank-you cards to and who was bringing the family dinner on which night.

I know I'm annoying/freaking out Mom. I keep laughing for no reason, giggly squeals that even I know are irritating. My leg is wiggling, and I can't tell if it's wiggling on its own or if I'm making it wiggle, but it is shaking Mom's chair. "Am I annoying you or freaking you out?" I ask her.

She sighs. "You're nervous," she says. "You get like this."

A nurse calls my name, and I look up and nod. I'm not even in the operating room yet, don't even know what it looks like, but she has a tiny paper cup in her hand and gives it to me. "Something to help you sleep," she says.

It's purple. It tastes like grape Kool-Aid and NyQuil and Theraflu. It's disgusting.

But it does the trick.

This is my worst time waking up. I wake to pure blackness. I can't open my eyes, either of them. I wait a little bit, like maybe I'm still half asleep or something because I don't remember anything after drinking the Kool-Aid. Maybe I'm too weak to open my eyes. Or maybe the surgery hasn't started?

As I come to in stages, I know it's already happened. I don't feel pain, not yet, but I feel a buzzing inside. I know something that was broken is fixed now, but it feels like the opposite. And there's still this thick, unnatural blackness.

I wait. There are no sounds. The faint beep of a monitor is maybe, *maybe*, off in the distance, but my mind could be making that up. I wait. I think: *Maybe my eyes* are *open.* I think about how they were peeling down my face, how my eyes are part of my face, how I never asked about what would happen to my eyes during the operation, because I didn't ask any questions. I didn't want to hear the answers.

So maybe my eyes *are* open. Maybe something went horribly, horribly wrong. Maybe something detached in my eyeballs when they were pulling things down or pulling them back up, and now I can't see anymore.

Maybe I've gone blind.

I've never known someone who was blind. I wonder what they see, if it's this same blackness I see. Or what if they can make out shapes and figures, and my kind of blindness isn't the same as a natural, organic blindness? What if my kind of blindness only occurs when your face gets mauled and then stapled back to the top of your head like it's no big deal?

What will I do now? I'm a writer. Miss Beck even said it. If I can't see, I can't write. I know there's Braille, but I don't know how you write in it. How do the dots get raised up like that? Why haven't I wondered about this before? Braille makes no sense!

Everything is still so quiet, like I'm in a tomb. A tomb. Is that where I am? Am I *dead*? *Heavenly Father*, I ask, because maybe I should have asked it a long time ago, *am I dead? If I'm dead, where are you?* Or is this hell—this black, this eternal darkness?

What did I do to end up in hell? The usual suspects come to mind, the sins I repent for on a regular basis: the hitting/kicking/scratching/various violence, of course, but I thought I'd been better about that. I don't like church. I forget to read my scriptures all the time. Is that enough to get me here?

Rembrandt. Rembrandt is technically a lie, isn't he? He feels so real, but he isn't, and the deepest, saddest part of me knows that. But he's so good. Could a lie so good damn me to hell?

Earth moves beneath me. It trembles and shakes, and judgment is here. *"Heavenly Father? Please help me."*

"You're okay, sweetie," says a voice. It's a woman's voice. The voice sounds too human to be God's voice, I think, but what do I know about God's voice? When I hear His still, small voice, I know it's only inside me. This voice is outside me.

"Shh," her voice says. "You're okay. Go back to sleep."

I'm rolling, I realize. I'm on a gurney, and I'm rolling. I was praying aloud. Someone is rolling me on this gurney and heard me mumbling a prayer, and she said, *You're okay, sweetie, shh, you're okay, go back to sleep.* Earth isn't trembling or shaking, I'm rolling, and judgment isn't here, just this doctor or nurse is.

"I'm awake!" I tell her, shout at her like *Hallelujah!* "I'm wide awake, but my eyes won't open!"

The rolling stops. "I couldn't hear you, sweetheart. What did you say?" Her warm breath touches my face, she's that close.

"I can't open my eyes?" I ask, meeker now that I know she's right here.

"Oh," she says. "No, you won't be able to for a few days at least. Lots of swelling after this kind of operation."

"Swelling?"

"Oh yeah, your eyes are swollen to slits right now. And the rest of your face? Puffed up like a balloon." She laughs, like it's funny, this idea of my face as a balloon.

I can't even smile. I'm not blind? I'm not dead?

The rolling starts back up. "The swelling will go down with time, though, just like a balloon. Can you hear me, Emily? You gotta give it time."

DISCHARGED

WHAT IT SAYS:
DISCHARGE/TRANSFER TO: Home

PRINCIPAL DIAGNOSIS:
1. Closed head injury secondary to auto-pedestrian accident—frontal orbital fracture; 2. Posterior fossa cystic astrocytoma

SECONDARY DIAGNOSIS:
Cerebrospinal fluid rhinorrhea

OPERATIONS/PROCEDURES: Posterior fossa craniotomy; tumor resection; frontal reconstructive surgery; bifrontal craniotomy with repair of dural defect using frontal sinus obliteration; cranial fixation of frontal bone fracture

PATIENT CONDITION: Satisfactory

Dear Parent,
These are the instructions you are to follow after you leave the hospital. Please read them carefully. If there is anything you do not understand, ask the physician or nurse.

ACTIVITY: As able. No bicycle riding, roller-skating, ice-skating, or other activities where potential for falling is high.

DIET: For age

FOLLOW-UP CARE: Medical staple removal post-op days 10–14, MRI post-op months 2–3. Outpatient physical therapy 2–3x per week for work on balance and coordination. Medications: Ferrous sulfate 325 mg by mouth 3x per day; Colace 100 mg by mouth 3x per day.

WHAT IT SHOULD SAY:
DISCHARGE/TRANSFER TO: A home that will be
completely different from the one you left, making you
question what *home* even means.

PRINCIPAL DIAGNOSIS:
1. Front of head smashed into a windshield; 2. Back of
head housed a bunch of stuff that shouldn't be there.

SECONDARY DIAGNOSIS:
Teeny-tiny cracks in front of head that nobody knew
about until spinal fluid started leaking out of your nose.

OPERATIONS/PROCEDURES: Stitched up the bloody
mess of forehead and took out the tumor, then found out about
the teeny-tiny cracks, so to fix them, they pulled the skin on
your face down and superglued the bones back together.

PATIENT CONDITION: How do you think?

> Dear Patient,
> These are the instructions to follow after you leave
> the hospital. They will not help you at all. Reading
> them carefully will make you think, *Duh, I knew
> that already.* Because, duh, you do. It's been your life
> for the last three months. If there is anything you
> do not understand, that's to be expected. Nobody
> knows what to expect, least of all the physicians and
> nurses. Recovery could be routine. Or something

could happen that no one saw coming. Your life is, as it has always been, anybody's guess.

ACTIVITY: Unlikely

DIET: Anything and everything—you might want to watch that.

FOLLOW-UP CARE: TBD

REMBRANDT'S SECOND LETTER

DEAR JOHANNA,
DON'T WORRY ABOUT TAKING A LONG TIME TO
WRITE ME BACK, B/C IT WOULD HAVE TAKEN ME
A LONG TIME TO ANSWER, EVEN IF THERE HAD
BEEN SOME WAY FOR ME TO GET YOUR LETTER.
EVERYTHING WITH EM WAS SO WEIRD, RIGHT? I
WAS REALLY DEVASTATED THERE FOR A WHILE. I
ONLY VISITED HER ONCE IN THE HOSPITAL AND
SHE SEEMED TO BE DOING BETTER, BUT I HAVEN'T
SEEN HER AT ALL SINCE SHE'S BEEN HOME. ANYWAY,
I KNOW YOU GUYS DON'T REALLY HANG OUT
ANYMORE, SO I WON'T GO ON AND ON ABOUT IT.

YOU SAY YOUR FAMILY'S BORING, BUT I THINK IT
SOUNDS COOL. I DON'T HAVE ANY BROTHERS AND

SISTERS, AND I WONDER WHAT IT WOULD BE LIKE TO HAVE PEOPLE AROUND BEING CRAZY ALL THE TIME. WHO DO YOU GET ALONG WITH THE BEST, AND WHO DO YOU FIGHT WITH THE MOST?

TO ANSWER YOUR QUESTION, I'M IN EIGHTH GRADE. MY SCHOOL IS SIXTH, SEVENTH, AND EIGHTH GRADE, SO I WILL GO TO HIGH SCHOOL NEXT YEAR, WHICH KINDA FREAKS ME OUT IN A WAY BUT MOSTLY IS A GOOD THING BECAUSE MIDDLE SCHOOL IS SOMETIMES LAME. MY FAVORITE CLASS IS ART. I JUST TAKE A REGULAR "ADVANCED ART" CLASS HERE, BUT NEXT YEAR I GET TO TAKE PHOTOGRAPHY, SO I AM PSYCHED ABOUT THAT.

PEACE.

REMBRANDT

P.S. THANKS FOR SAYING YOU LIKE MY HANDWRITING.

P.P.S. DON'T WORRY ABOUT YOUR SPELLING. I DEFINITELY THINK IT SHOWS CREATIVITY TO BE ABLE TO SPELL A WORD MORE THAN ONE WAY.

P.P.P.S. I REALIZED MAYBE YOU MEANT WHAT IS

MY FAVORITE CLASS BESIDES ART, AND THAT IS
FRENCH. ALMOST ALL THE GUYS TAKE IT B/C THE
TEACHER, MLLE. ROQUET, IS HOT. BUT I JUST LIKE IT.

P.P.P.P.S. THANKS FOR THE NEW PIC OF YOURSELF. I
AGREE, YOU LOOK A LOT OLDER NOW.

P.P.P.P.P.S. I WILL FIND A PIC OF MYSELF TO SHOW
YOU.

P.P.P.P.P.P.S. REIGNING P.S. CHAMPION!!!

THE BIG DAY

It's my first Big Day.

I'm sick of hearing it. Before I was even chosen to go to the District Writing Festival, back when I'd only asked Dad to type up my entry, he took the spiral notebook out of my hands, nodded, and said, "What's this for?" He knows I only want my manuscripts typed if there's a specific reason.

"A contest," I told him. "I want to go to the District Writing Festival again." Each spring, my school district hosts a writing festival. Two kids from each elementary school are selected to go based on the writing sample they submit. I went to the festival last year, too, and that time I wrote a story about a girl who moved to a new school and how she learned to fit in there.

This year, I wrote about the accident. I called it "The Road to Recovery." It's sappy. I know it will win.

Dad remembers last year, because he says, "Are you sure, Em? It's a Big Day."

That's the point. It's a big, extraordinary Saturday starting early in the morning. You get to go to a high school and sit in an auditorium with real upholstered seats that swing up when no one's in them. You get to listen to writers talk about how important writing is, and you know that even if other kids don't care about what you can do, *you're* right to care about it. You go to a classroom with no dumb alphabet chart on the wall reminding you how to write a capital *Q* in cursive. The walls have posters on them with profound quotes by famous people. You sit in a circle and all the kids read their writing and everyone claps at the end. There's a snack break with cookies. There's pizza for lunch.

And then. Then you get to meet authors. Authors who live among us, right here in Utah. They talk about the books they've written or the magazines they've been published in, and they tell the stories behind their stories, and for that moment, being an author is more than a dream. It's close enough to touch.

It is a Big Day in the best way.

Later that week, when I hand in my submission to Miss Beck, she looks at it, then at me, and says: "Really, Emily? It's a Big Day."

She does not say it like it's a Big Day in the best way.

Miss Beck, too? Miss Beck thinks I can't handle a Big Day?

Since the accident, no one wants me to have a Big Day. No one wants me to do anything. I know it's because I came home in a wheelchair, but that was only for a few days, for long distances, and I didn't really need it. And I have to leave school early or come late a lot of days, but that's mostly because of doctor appointments or physical therapy or the orthodontist. Sometimes it's because I'm tired, or because my headache is whirling too fast for me to keep myself up, but that hardly ever happens.

Now that I can't do them, even the things I didn't used to want to do sound appealing. The kids play softball in PE, and I know I'd hate it if I *had* to join in. But when I don't *get* to join in, when I have to sit there and watch on the hill by myself, I long to stand in line and wait for my turn at bat, looking bored like the others. I want to go out at recess, but instead I stay in so I don't slip on the thawing ice or get run into by an overzealous four-square player.

I get to have someone stay in with me at recess, a "buddy." At first, everybody wanted a turn, people who weren't my friends before the accident and aren't really my friends now.

Most of the time, Johanna stays in with me. I used to think she liked it, because she hates recess, and it was still cold and icy outside with gray snow everywhere, and sometimes kids would still ask her why she wasn't hanging out with Kacie and Jess anymore, and she said it got annoying.

But now it's almost spring, and it's warmer, and we've already talked about everything we can possibly talk about without mentioning the accident. She doesn't want to talk about anything even remotely related to it. Not what happened that night. Not Damien or Damien's dad. Not what happened all those days after in the hospital. Not the headaches and the woozy-head I have now. I read her crystal clear.

We talk about junior high coming up, because that's the only thing Johanna *does* want to talk about. Already, we can see minor tears in the long-standing elementary school best-friend couplings: Amanda and Tiffany, Veronica and Laura.

"A split is bound to happen," Johanna says as we're putting together the United States jigsaw puzzle for the hundredth time. "People grow up. That's how it was with me and Kacie and Jess. That's how it is for a lot of friendships."

Is that how it is for her and Rembrandt? Is a split bound to happen there? If she doesn't write to him anymore, she won't have to give me the letters to give to him, and I might not get to see her at all.

"And what about us?" Johanna runs her fingers over the long, narrow body of Tennessee before wedging it in between Kentucky and Alabama. "We probably won't have any classes together. Will we even be *friends* in junior high?"

And by the way she says it, I know. I know she isn't pondering whether or not we will be friends in junior high. She is *counting* on us not being friends in junior high.

Johanna and me, we were over long before the Mounds bar.

—

So the District Writing Festival is tomorrow and it's hard not to feel like all I have is this Big Day. Mom says, "Better get some sleep. Tomorrow is a Big Day." And I grind my teeth and count to ten, and I go to my room and I do not throw anything.

The writing festival school is far enough away that on the drive there, my dad reminds me of the rules multiple times. "Take a break if you get tired. Call us if you need to come home. Always hold on to the railing going up or down stairs."

Pointless rules. I can't *go* up or down stairs without holding on to a railing, even if I wanted to. Of course I'll call if I need to come home. And take a break if I get tired from *what*? This isn't a marathon.

I slide into an upholstered auditorium seat and swing my legs. An editor from *Salt Lake* magazine talks about how important writing is. I go into a classroom with posters on the wall that read ARTISTS ARE SUBCONSCIOUS PHILOSOPHERS and A LEAF FALLS. HISTORY IS MADE. I don't know what subject is taught in this room, but I know it must be deep. We sit in a circle and everyone reads their writing and the kids can't believe that my story is true and they clap extra loud at the end. I have a chocolate-chunk cookie during snack break. I have pineapple-and-Canadian-bacon pizza at lunch.

And then. Then I get to meet the authors. And that is when I meet her.

Her name is Louise Plummer. She's written two books for sale here at the festival, and I've read them both, twice. One was in the young adult paperback section of the library face out, so I checked it out. And as I read it, I couldn't believe it was there, in writing, the story of someone who felt the way I did. So I read the other one, too. Then I read them again.

Louise Plummer. I didn't know she lived here, in Utah, among us, among *me*. I keep looking from her face to her book cover to her face again, and blinking. I am a cliché.

There's an autograph party at the end of the day, the Big Day, but I'm not too tired to wait for Louise Plummer to sign the book I bought (I could only afford one).

"Hello, there," Louise says when it's my turn. She looks at my name tag.

"I love your books," I tell her. "I can't believe you're here. I can't believe you feel the same way I do." *Stupid, stupid, stupid.*

"Thank you," she says, ignoring my customary bad opening statement, my shaking Bad Hand, my tousled bad hair. She pauses. "You're a real writer, I can tell."

I smile at her, shy and small so I don't broadcast my braces.

She opens the book to the title page and creases it.

"I like your other book better, but I bought this one because it's checked out of the library more often."

Louise laughs. I love the way Louise laughs. If I become an author, will I learn to laugh that way? She laughs like something bad might have happened to her in the past, but it doesn't matter now.

To Emily, she writes. *Someday I'll be reading you in print—and I'll be cheering! Love, Louise Plummer.*

Sixth-grade graduation ensemble, complete with hat.

THE NEXT GRADUATION DAY

"Welcome, students . . . please sit down. Mrs. Wright's class, flat on pockets. Mrs. Wright's class, *sit down*."

Funny how nobody listens to her. Funny how she actually believes we'll pay attention just because she's the principal.

"Thank you, students. Thank you. Today is an exciting day for South Midvalley Elementary School—an exciting, proud day. Today, we recognize the outstanding achievements of our students throughout this school year. Today, our sixth graders will be graduating to junior high."

It's the last-day-of-school awards ceremony, a South Midvalley Elementary tradition. All those other last-day-of-schools, while I sat cross-legged on the dusty gym/lunchroom floor, with some smelly classmate humming in my ear or cracking his knuckles, I was waiting patiently, biding my time until *this* last day of school.

Funny, how it's exactly like I imagined it would be and nothing like I imagined it would be. Funny how much of my life ends up this way: left field unexpected with enough mundane to rein it back into reality.

"We've had a great year, haven't we, folks?"

She says this every year. She always calls us folks. She always looks over at the sixth graders, who are sitting on the stage steps instead of the floor, and she always winks. Funny, how stupid it is, but how much I want her to do it this year. Wink and leave it at that, the same way she does every year. She doesn't.

"It has also been a challenging year for some of you, full of trials met with courage!"

She is looking at me. Everybody in the audience who wasn't already looking at me follows her stare to find me. Little kids with wide eyes, middle kids with bug eyes, older kids with rolled eyes. They've all seen me before. Everyone knows the Thank-God-She-Got-Hit-By-A-Car Girl. I'm the only kid in school allowed to wear a hat. I wear a hat every day, to cover up the hair sprouting like new radishes in patches on my head.

Funny, how I've spent my entire elementary school career dreaming of this last day of school. Because I was the smart girl, the brainy girl, the girl who would win all the awards, and if I didn't have friends, well, at least I had certificates and ribbons and a plaque. So I dreamed of the sixth-grade awards ceremony, when all eyes would be on me.

Funny how that dream is coming true, how all eyes are on me now, but not because I'm sweeping the place clean of awards. Funny how it's because I'm wearing a hat.

"Let's give a big hand to our sixth graders, who have all met challenges—some small, some *life-changing*. For some, simply surviving this year has been a triumph."

Funny how she thinks she's being subtle. Everyone knows she's talking about me, the girl who won't be winning any awards today, because she spent most of this year in bed instead of in school.

What none of them know is that I'm not the smart girl anymore, that even when I get better, I won't really be better. My head has been squished and picked at and rebuilt, and I've survived this year, but my brain hasn't. Funny how foreign but distinct it feels, not to be smart when I once was.

"Let's hear it for our sixth-grade class, who will continue to be bright, confident leaders as they move on to seventh grade!"

Funny, how little I believe her.

JUNIOR HIGH JENNIFER

Jennifer is a skank. She has a wide, too-loose walk and narrow hips with too-tight jeans.

I don't know this when I ask her to be my locker partner on the first day of seventh grade.

When Jennifer sidles into my first-period math class ten minutes late, I don't see her because I'm staring straight ahead like I should be. There's been a bell. But class isn't starting, and instead of kids clowning around because class hasn't started, throwing paper airplanes and writing on the whiteboard and swearing because there's nobody telling them not to, everyone is quiet. Nikki and Alaina, the BFFs who've been chattering nonstop up until now, are silent. Even the teacher, Ms. Evans, isn't talking.

Every woman at this school is a *Ms*. No one is married or single. On the schedule, it made every name look more imposing. Each teacher seemed faceless, less human. But Ms. Evans is human. She wears dark nylons and a navy scarf tied in a knot that tries to be a knot but isn't. She's *too* human. She's as scared as I am. Maybe more.

Probably not more.

I uncurl the computer printout in my hand one more time. My class schedule. I'm so afraid of losing it that I've kept it in my fist since I got to school this morning, since I scanned the halls looking for my classroom like I was stuck in a bad dream, since I saw that all the other students in this class seemed to know someone, at least one person.

I don't know anyone. Not one person.

I rehearse my schedule, try to visualize the order of classes and where the rooms are so I don't have to check when class gets out. After math there's French, then chorus, then lunch. Gifted and Talented in the afternoon.

Gifted and Talented isn't exactly a class. From what my orientation letter said, it's a group of thirty seventh graders who take English, Utah Studies, and Life Science together every afternoon and work on "enrichment" projects every semester.

We had to take a test to get into Gifted and Talented. It was administered last year when I was still in the hospital, but they offered me a chance to take it when I got out.

I was terrified of taking the test. Even then, before I had been back to school, before I knew it for sure, I was afraid I wasn't smart anymore. Afraid that even my "brainy loser" trademark would no longer fit. Afraid that now I had *nothing* left.

I'd noticed it while reading my first book postsurgery, a novel my uncle had given me about a girl trying to grow an award-winning pumpkin. At first I didn't realize how long I was spending on each word, each paragraph, each page. Once I did, I chalked it up to being tired. Every day, I chalked it up to being tired. Then finally: Maybe this is how long it takes me to read now.

And if I didn't read like I used to, was it a guarantee I did anything like I used to?

It wasn't. Back at school, I still got tired all the time and wrote slower and got so frustrated I wanted to push and kick and hit somebody, and sometimes I did, but no one told on me, because I was the Thank-God-She-Got-Hit-By-A-Car Girl.

I passed the test. Only because they gave me extra time. But I passed the test.

I wonder if Johanna passed the test—if Johanna will be in Gifted and Talented, too. I wonder if she'll talk to me. She hasn't talked to me all summer, but that's not a surprise.

At least there's Rembrandt. Without Rembrandt, I wouldn't even know Johanna still exists, but she sends him letters by giving them to me or mailing them to my house, and she doesn't write about me in the letters, but at least I have some small piece of her still.

I shift in my seat. Waiting is worse in junior high desks. I hate junior high desks. Instead of elementary school desks that are square, junior high desks are missing a chunk where I'm supposed to put my elbow. The only armrest is on the other side, where I don't need one.

Every desk is like this. Right-handed.

Finally, Ms. Evans says: "Okay." Maybe she did deep breathing or counted to ten slowly or one of the other techniques the doctors taught me for controlling anxiety. "I know you guys aren't going to listen to anything I say until you get your locker. So go ahead, choose a partner."

Everyone else is pairing up with whatever kid they already know—or their best friend, in the case of Nikki and Alaina—and this end-of-the-world panic washes over me. This is about survival of the fittest, and if I don't get a locker partner ASAP, I'll be the weakest link or the missing link or however that goes.

There's one girl I didn't see before class. She doesn't have a locker partner yet. I remember what Mom told me about making friends, how you can't just sit around and wait for them to come to you. You have to put yourself out there, join clubs and groups, talk to people. "Take the initiative," Mom said.

I take the initiative and say to the girl behind me, "Hi, I'm Emily. What's your name?"

She has red hair, but it's light, and she has freckles like I do, but they're subtle. "Jennifer," she says. She smiles. She doesn't smile like a seventh grader. She smiles slow, sultry and mysterious, but the smile looks like it belongs on her face.

"Do you know anybody in this class?"

She shakes her head lazy; turning it slow to one side, slow to the other side. "I just got here. I slept in this morning."

I didn't. I didn't even *sleep* this morning. I don't know what time it was when I woke up, listing things that could go wrong, second-guessing my wardrobe selection of stonewashed jeans and a tapestry vest, wishing I were back in the hospital, where it sucked but at least the pain was the easy kind I knew how to handle.

Who oversleeps on the first day of junior high?

"Seriously," I say. "*Way* too early." But enough talk. Back to business. "I don't know anyone in this class, either." I want her to know I wouldn't be asking this if I knew anybody else. I want her to know I'm not so despised that the people who know me don't want to share with me. Even if that might be true. "So do you want to be locker partners?"

And her shrug is like everything about her: one shoulder lifts and falls; it takes its time. "Sure, I guess."

Ours is locker #666. The combination is 10-20-30 and when Jennifer spins the dial and lifts the handle, it opens easily. When I try, not so much.

"Do you have a boyfriend?" she asks while I'm giving it another spin. Ms. Evans says we should all open the locker at least once so we know that it's working.

I think of Rembrandt. "No, not really. Just a guy who's a friend."

"I do," says Jennifer. "Bronco. He's a ninth grader."

I lift the handle. The door doesn't open.

"Weird," she says. "Let me try again, to make sure I didn't bust it." Spin, lift, swing. She didn't bust it.

Most of the kids are back in class by now. Jennifer takes something out of her backpack while I keep spinning. "I don't smoke, but Bronco asked me to hold these for him."

I look over my shoulder to make sure she's talking about what I think she's talking about. Yep. Cigarettes. Great. We're a tobacco-free campus, and the administration acts like it's the World's Biggest Deal. If they find you in possession, it's automatic suspension.

"It's cool if I keep them in here, right?"

I lift the handle. Nothing. "Here's the deal," I say, a joke to keep from crying. "You get the locker open, you can put anything in it you want." Because I know she will anyway.

Jennifer nods a slow, in-no-hurry nod. "Cool. I think this is gonna be a pretty good year."

ANOTHER LETTER FROM REMBRANDT

DEAR JOHANNA,
DID YOU NOTICE HOW OUR LETTERS WERE
BECOMING ONE LONG P.S. CHAIN? THIS YEAR IS
ALREADY OUT OF CONTROL, AND THE ONLY TIME
I HAVE TO WRITE IS IN STUDY HALL, AND I CAN'T
REMEMBER WHAT P.S. WE ARE UP TO, SO I DECLARE
IT A TRUCE. WHAT DO YOU SAY?

HIGH SCHOOL IS AWESOME BUT SO BUSY. I LOVE
MY PHOTOGRAPHY CLASS, BUT I AM REALIZING
MY CAMERA KINDA SUCKS. I'M TAKING A
DRAWING CLASS NEXT SEMESTER THAT YOU
USUALLY HAVE TO BE A SOPHOMORE TO TAKE,
BUT THE TEACHER IS MY PHOTOGRAPHY TEACHER,
SO HE'S LETTING ME IN. YOU WILL BE SAD TO

KNOW THE FRENCH TEACHER HERE IS A DUDE
SO YOU CAN NO LONGER MOCK ME ABOUT ONLY
TAKING FRENCH B/C OF THE HOT TEACHER.
NOW YOU CAN BE ASSURED OF MY DEEP LOVE FOR
THE FRENCH LANGUAGE, HA-HA.

HOW IS JUNIOR HIGH? EM SAYS IT IS CRAZY BUSY
IN THAT SPECIAL GIFTED CLASS OR WHATEVER
IT IS. YOU TWO ARE TOO SMART FOR ME. DO YOU
MOSTLY HANG OUT WITH THE KIDS IN THAT
CLASS? MY FRIENDS ARE MOSTLY THE OTHER ART
KIDS, BUT I HANG OUT WITH OTHER PEOPLE, TOO,
LIKE ADRIANNA EVEN THOUGH I DON'T SEE HER
AS MUCH B/C SHE'S STILL AT THE MIDDLE SCHOOL.
AND EM WHO I ONLY SEE ON WEEKENDS B/C SHE
LIVES BY YOU. I WISH SHE LIVED HERE, BUT THEN
I GUESS I WOULD NEVER HAVE STARTED WRITING
TO YOU. IT'S GOOD THAT YOU TWO STILL HAVE
SOME CLASSES TOGETHER SO SHE CAN BRING ME
YOUR LETTERS.

WELL, THE BELL IS GOING TO RING IN LIKE 30
SECONDS SO I BETTER SIGN OFF FOR NOW.

PEACE.

REMBRANDT

UNISON

I have seventh-grade Soprano/Alto Chorus right before lunch. We have chorus partners because there's not enough of anything in this school to go around, including sheet music. I hate my chorus partner. She's an idiot. Her name is Brittany.

Brittany will always grab the music, as if I don't exist, and then hold it away from me. It's as though we are not partners who must share music, but as though everyone else in class has a partner with whom they must share music, but she does not.

I'm sick of it, so I decide to get our music before she has a chance to take it from me. The next day, I arrive early, but Brittany's already grabbed our green music folder from its cubby. Brittany is always on time to class, even though she is popular so she should be late from talking to her friends.

This angers me. I don't have any friends to talk to between classes, but I can never get my locker to open once I find it, and the chorus room is in the K hall, the music hall far away from everything except the gym and the cafeteria, and I always scootch in right before the final bell. It's not fair.

And Brittany is tipping back on her chair while she sings "I Enjoy Being a Girl," and I want her to fall, but I know she won't, and this makes me madder. Ms. Goates is pounding away on the piano, hitting each key harder than the last, like she's hoping to drown us out. I know the words to "I Enjoy Being a Girl" because we've sung it before. I don't like the words or particularly want to read them, but I can't stand how everyone else is looking at the words and I am singing them from memory, like some wannabe who tries too hard. So I tug the sheet music in my direction.

Brittany tugs it back.

I tug it again. "I can't see," I hiss while we're supposed to hold the note from the first *girl*.

"Then look harder," she says, rolling her eyes like *duh*.

"No!" I say, and elbow her. "I want it where I can see it, too."

And I swear, *I swear*, she elbows me back. And does not move the music.

Naturally, I kick her. In the ankle, because the elbowing seems to have had no effect, so it falls on me to escalate. She says "Ow," and I say "Lemme see the music," but she doesn't, so I pinch a narrow bit of the flesh right below her short sleeve. I know that will make her drop the music and she does, automatically, into my outstretched hand. She says "Freak!" and I say "You're supposed to share the music! Everyone else here is *sharing music!*"

Ms. Goates stops playing and says, "What's going on?"

"We're supposed to share the music." I point at Brittany.

"She was hurting me." Brittany points at me.

"You were hurting me, too."

"You *pinched* me!"

"We're supposed to share music!"

Ms. Goates scoots out her piano bench, which she never does before the song is over, even if someone is at the door waiting for her. But this song is not over and Ms. Goates says, "We're going to sing 'La Bamba' next, so get that out of your folders and talk quietly." No one talks quietly, but everyone gets out "La Bamba."

And Ms. Goates takes Brittany to the little office attached to the room, the one that locks, for what I presume is a talking-to about how we have to share music, even if our chorus partner is ugly and unpopular and her breath always has a weirdness to it, no matter how often she brushes her teeth, no matter how much Scope and floss she uses. How we might not bother to remember her name, but that doesn't mean we don't have to share music with her, because we're supposed to share music.

Brittany comes out of the office, and someone asks, "What did Ms. Goates say?" I'm *right there,* and Brittany shrugs and says, "I guess that girl has brain damage or something." Because Brittany never remembers my name.

The next day, everybody changes chorus partners, not just me, but I know it's because of me. My new partner's name is Candace, and we each hold one side of the sheet music. I use my left hand even though my right one is closer, even though it makes turning pages awkward. We share music, just like we are supposed to.

NEUROPSYCHOLOGICAL EVALUATION

Emily Wing
Age: 13 years, 2 months
Examiner: Maria K. Halestrom, MS
Doctoral student in school psychology

REASON FOR REFERRAL:

Assess Emily's current level of intellectual and cognitive ability as well as her neurobehavioral status post–head injury and brain surgery.

BACKGROUND INFORMATION:

Emily is the oldest of five children, with two bothers (one age four and one age eight) and two sisters (one age ten and one age three months). Her mother is a homemaker and her father is an attorney. Early developmental motor milestones appeared to be age appropriate. Mrs. Wing described Emily as a bright child but one who was easily frustrated and quick to anger. She was very creative and enjoyed making elaborate "sculptures" with discarded items. Her temper and frustration level, however, were of concern to the Wings. Her mother also noted concern regarding Emily's high anxiety level, which she became aware of at approximately age four. Emily would sometimes become hysterical when her creative projects did not turn out as she expected them to.

Although Mr. and Mrs. Wing did not recall any difficulty for Emily in learning to walk, she has always had difficulty with coordination and clumsiness. She experienced problems with gross motor activities such as bouncing a ball, jumping rope, and dancing. However, she likes to draw and has produced finely detailed drawings. Emily still has to stop and think when figuring out directions (right from left). She also had difficulty learning to tell time and counting money.

Emily has worn corrective lenses since age seven. She has a history of headaches and balance problems.

Since the head injury, Emily's sense of smell has changed. She experiences "phantom smells." Her headaches continue. Crowds, noise, and movement now distract her, and her concentration in general is diminished. Emily has a tremor in the right hand.

Her father reports that she is doing better physically over the last year but seems more depressed and frustrated. It is of some concern to Mr. Wing that Emily used to read books all the time but does not do so now. This may be because, according to Emily, reading intensifies her headaches and general wooziness.

Emily has had difficulty with peer relationships. She relates well to older people but often feels that kids her own age don't like her. She tends to have an introspective temperament and keeps to herself. She is also described as morose. Mrs. Wing reported that Emily told her she has always been unhappy. Since the accident/surgery, she seems even more depressed and frustrated. Emily is currently seeing a psychologist, as she has intermittently since age six.

Since entering elementary school, Emily has always been an excellent student. She has always been in "gifted and talented" programs, and there has been no alternative for her but an A. Schoolwork seemed to be easy for her, however Emily displayed considerable anxiety to maintain high grades and gain approval from the teacher. Along with the excellent grades have come tears, insecurity, and fear of failure. Emily's strengths have always been in reading and writing.

After the accident and removal of her tumor, Emily has had a much higher frustration level. Things that were easy for her before are much harder now. She spends an inordinate amount of time on her schoolwork and becomes easily fatigued.

APPEARANCE AND BEHAVIORAL OBSERVATIONS:
Emily, an attractive young lady with brown hair and glasses, presented for testing casually dressed and well groomed. She is of average height and weight.

She is left-handed. Her left-handedness has been evident from a very young age. Emily displayed a generally positive affect; however, she displayed "intense" behavior when working on tasks.

TEST RESULTS AND INTERPRETATIONS:

While Emily's full-scale IQ score falls in the "high average range," the discrepancy between her verbal and performance test scores is dramatic and highly significant. She had difficulty with performance subtests, more visual/spatial in nature, and used only her left hand during the object assembly task.

SUMMARY AND RECOMMENDATIONS:

Because of the complications of interaction between the injury and the tumor, it is difficult to sort out the relative contributions of each as they relate to Emily's current functioning and the difficulty she is experiencing. What is evident is that she is having much more difficulty in her academic work than she was a year ago. It is also clear that Emily's anxiety and frustration level, while always high, has increased since her accident. Some of this is likely related to the trauma as well as the uncertainty with which she most likely views life. This is not surprising, given the serious medical problems she has experienced.

Since it appears that Emily continues to experience high levels of depression and anxiety, continued counseling focused on these issues is important. Group therapy may be a consideration.

As Emily has experienced some difficulty with peer relationships, involvement with other groups with young people is recommended. It would be helpful if Emily could find a few peers who share common interests with whom she can feel comfortable. Because of her significant skill and talent as a writer, a writing class at a community college or the University of Utah extension is highly recommended.

It is suggested that Emily be evaluated again in roughly twelve months to monitor her ongoing recovery and obtain a clearer picture of long-term residuals to her neurological problems.

Trying to be social. I've decided that's the next step to becoming well.

ASHLEY'S HOUSE

This is how it started out. I sat behind Crystal in French. She turned backward, looked me in the eye, and said: "Will you be my friend?"

It's the summer after seventh grade, and I still haven't learned the difference between school-friends and friends-you-hang-out-with-friends. Crystal wrote her number in my yearbook. She wrote, *Have a bitchin' summer! Call me!* And I didn't realize that seventh graders—seventh graders other than me—wrote the same thing in everyone's yearbook.

I'm a slow learner.

So it's two weeks into June and I'm trying to be social because I've decided that's the next step to becoming well. And Crystal was the one who asked to be my friend.

Crystal has plans to hang out with her friend Ashley today, but she invites me along. She says to meet her at

Smith's at one thirty. We never buy groceries at Smith's, because it's far away and not in a great neighborhood. When my mom drops me off, Crystal and Ashley are there already, straddling their bikes and laughing at something.

"Where's your bike?" asks Ashley. I've never met Ashley, but she has a look like maybe I've seen her before. She's not exactly pretty (her nose is sharp, sort of like a beak), but she has long dark hair and a willowy body. An everyone-should-know-me look radiates off her.

"I live too far away to bike," I say, and it's true, but not really an answer. I don't have a bike. I haven't had a bike in years. Since way before the accident, I haven't had a bike.

I outgrew my starter bike, the one that took me forever to learn to ride, and I never asked for another. I've never liked bikes. Riding a bike made me all tipsy-turvy even before the accident. I can't imagine what I'd be like now.

They walk their bikes and I follow them behind Smith's and down a road I never knew existed. Ashley's talking about her boyfriend, Eric, and how he might show up today but sometimes he's such an effing loser but sometimes he's so effing sweet. Crystal and Eric go way back because he lives "upstairs," and she keeps nodding and laughing and saying: "Yep, yep, all true."

We're taking a jaunt to Ashley's house to show Crystal that Ashley does, indeed, have a three-story tree house in her backyard. And this is why I'll never understand junior high: because Crystal is joking about Eric's "teeny-tiny dick" while she's all excited about seeing a *tree house*.

How did I get here? It's clear that Ashley's somebody

popular and so, by extension, Crystal is also somebody popular, and one of these things is not like the others, and I don't belong here. But how was I supposed to know? Crystal talked to me first. Crystal was the one to ask: "Will you be my friend?"

Ashley gathers her T-shirt fabric up above her belly button and twists it. "Eff, it's hot." She tries to tie what she's twisted, but it's not long enough, and it uncurls like it, too, is wilting in the heat.

I've never heard a person be as blasé as Ashley is while using the F-word this much. She's not mad or sad or on the brink of a meltdown. It's like using it in whatever form she can is all she has to make the conversation interesting.

It makes me feel bad for her in a way I can't quite figure out. But she's Popular and I'm Unpopular, so I'm not allowed to pity her.

Ashley's house isn't like I expect it to be. It has a picture of Jesus Christ in the front hallway that's the same picture all too-cute Mormon families have in their front hallway. I didn't expect Ashley to be from a too-cute Mormon family.

Ashley pats down her T-shirt so that you can't tell it was twisted up. It doesn't matter, though, because the only person home is her high school–age brother watching TV on the couch, and he doesn't even notice we're there.

Outside, we see it: the three-story tree house. Climbing up is tricky for me, but I think I do okay (who ever heard of building a three-story tree house without stairs?), until I hoist myself up and Ashley says, "Took you long enough!" and Crystal opens her eyes wide like, *Uh, yeah.* The tree house is pretty cool, I guess, but I don't pay too much attention, because I'm embarrassed for taking so long. And besides, it's hot. So we decide to go to Crystal's.

"You can ride my mom's bike," says Ashley, because I'm too tall for her little sister's. I wish I were shorter. Ashley's sister's pink bike with its white floral design reminds me of my last bike, and Ashley's mom's ten-speed freaks me out.

I'm not supposed to ride a bike without a helmet. Ever. But especially not at first, Dr. Walker says. In a couple of years, my head will grow hard again, but right now it's got soft spots, like a baby's.

But no one else is wearing a helmet, and when I ask if I can borrow one, Ashley raises an eyebrow, like *seriously?*, and says, "We don't have any helmets." And that's that.

The bike seat is too small, like it was carved out of a regular-sized bike seat. My bulges spill off either side. Ashley and Crystal speed away while I'm still getting my feet into the stirrups on the pedals.

I ride behind them like the tail of a misshapen kite. "You can ride up here with us," Crystal says kindly.

I try to joke. "If we ride three in a row, I'll get too close to traffic. Then all it takes is one little swerve and—bam— I'll get hit by a car again!"

"Again?" Crystal laughs. "When were you hit by a car *before?*"

I didn't know she didn't know.

I don't keep any of it secret, the accident or the brain tumor or the hospital.

Back in sixth grade, everyone knew. But now, in junior high, hardly anyone knows, and it's tricky. It can't be the first thing you tell other kids about yourself, because that's weird and it looks like you're trying to get sympathy.

This is how it started out. I sat behind Crystal in French. She turned backward, looked me in the eye, and said, "Will you be my friend?"

"Sure, I'm Emily. Last year I was hit by a car and doctors discovered I had a pre-existing brain tumor. That's why a chunk of my hair's gone. And look! You can still see the scars!"

Yeah. It can't go down like that.

"I got hit by a car in sixth grade," I tell Ashley and Crystal now. "I couldn't walk for a while. That's why I'm still getting used to riding a bike again." The abbreviated truth.

"You never forget how to ride a bike," says Ashley.

"Were you in a coma?" Crystal asks.

It's too hard to concentrate on talking and staying upright, and Crystal has slowed down anyway, so I get off the bike and walk it. "Um, I was unconscious?"

"It's the same thing," says Crystal, the sage.

And that's the last we talk about the accident.

CRYSTAL'S HOUSE

Crystal's house is exactly like I expect it to be. It's not a house; it's an apartment on the ground floor of a complex that reminds me of Driftwood Park. Beige. Creepy. The buildings all face a courtyard with too-long grass and dandelions.

"I'll be right back," says Crystal. "You guys wait out here." She doesn't let us go inside her house—not now, not later, not ever.

We sit on the grass, next to where we've laid our bikes. Ashley lies down. Back at her house, she changed into a white camisole, and now she pushes the straps off her shoulders. "I want my tan to get *so good* this summer."

It's probably not a direct dis, but it feels that way as I stare at my own legs. They're what people refer to as "pasty," but they don't remind me of paste. Ever since the accident, I've had these pinprick-sized pink dots all over my legs, and they seem to get brighter when I shave, like I did this morning. I got rid of the leg hair I'd been ignoring all summer in a marathon shaving session so I wouldn't be embarrassed. As if a razor were a magic wand that could stop the inevitable.

Years pass, my leg hair grows out, Ashley and I say nothing, and finally Crystal comes back, beaming. There's a lady next to her, young and thin, with reddish-blond hair. In a way, she looks like Crystal, even though Crystal's sort of squishy around the edges and her hair is more dish-water blond than red blond. The lady has a work outfit on: skirt, heels, shirt that buttons. She looks both at home here and completely out of place.

"This is my sister, Shawna. She's gonna take us to the Plaza."

Nothing about this makes sense. Crystal has a sister who's a grown-up? She wants to take us somewhere? This neighborhood has a *plaza*?

And what are we supposed to do with the bikes?

I just ask the last part.

Shawna smiles at me. No one's smiled at me all day. "Nobody's gonna mess with 'em." She jangles her keys. "Let's go."

Shawna's car is Slurpee-blue and has only two doors. I'm horrible at cars with two doors, at stumbling into the back, but I can't sit up front with Shawna; that's obviously Crystal's place. So I duck my head and crawl in after Ashley, hoping I don't collapse too close to her.

"I wish I didn't have to work," Shawna says to Crystal. "It's been forever since we got to hang out."

My sister and I avoid hanging out at all costs. Sitting next to each other at dinner is about all the hanging out we can muster.

"And your friends look so cute!"

This is where the bizarre takes a turn for the outright untrue. Ashley looks popular, not cute. I look like the "Before" picture on any number of infomercials.

For the first time, it occurs to me that I don't actually *know* any of these people, and as we get farther and farther from any place I've ever seen before, it occurs to me that this might be dangerous.

But everywhere is dangerous. Nowhere is safe.

Shawna pulls into a parking lot between two busy streets. "Have fun, girls!" To Crystal, she says: "You have money, right?" Crystal nods, but Shawna hands her a twenty-dollar bill anyway. "For an emergency only," she says, and Crystal nods solemnly.

The Plaza is air-conditioned. It's a smoky, dimly lit place with bar stools in the corner. Straight ahead there's a lounge with a hand-lettered sign: 21 OR OLDER! There's a CD-player jukebox, arcade games along one wall, and a pool table in the middle. "You guys play pool?" Crystal asks.

Ashley and I shake our heads.

"I'll teach you."

Pool is a game of precision, a game of both highly tuned fine-motor skills and sharp visual-spatial reasoning.

Guess how well I do.

"Let's play something else," says Crystal after a while. She's afraid I'm going to scratch the felt lining of the table and "the guys will kill us." Which sounds pretty bad.

"*Dr. Mario!*" says Ashley, so that's our next stop.

I wish they had *Ms. Pac-Man*. I'm terrible at video games, but they had a *Ms. Pac-Man* machine in the play-room at Children's Hospital, and when I was well enough, sometimes I'd play. I was pretty good, compared to sick kids who could barely use their limbs.

But they don't have *Ms. Pac-Man* here. It's not retro; it's old.

"Your turn," says Ashley.

Woo-hoo.

"I've never played this game before," I say to the surprise of no one while I fumble in my pocket for quarters.

"We'll show you what to do. It's easy," says Crystal, but she sounds unsure.

The game starts. The machine is the loudest and brightest part of the Plaza, making the stakes feel that much higher. I can't decide if I should use my good hand to control the joystick or the buttons.

"Put that yellow one there," says Crystal.

"Move the red one over—no, not that way, the other way," says Ashley.

"What are you doing?" says Crystal. "That's not right."

The game ends in, like, twenty seconds—probably an all-time low.

Finally Ashley asks what everyone, even me, has been

wondering all day: "So what are you *good* at?"

I take in a deep breath and think about what to say. I want to tell her the truth: I'm not good at anything. I never was. Then the brain tumor was removed and I should have gotten better, but it was mixed up with the car accident and my general *me*-ness, and all I know for sure is that I've only gotten worse.

But I can't say that. Even though it might make them sad, a little, and maybe they might soften toward me, a little. I've already brought up the accident once, and there were no takers. So I grasp at the only other straw I have. "I'm a good writer."

"What, like handwriting?" says Ashley.

"No, writing like stories and poems and articles for the school newspaper and stuff." Stuff like letters, technically from Rembrandt.

Their reaction to this information is like a seventh grader's reaction to another seventh grader being fluent in Latin: At some level they sense this should be impressive, but it isn't.

"Oh, so you're smart," says Crystal.

I'm not—not really, not anymore—so I shrug.

Crystal puzzles it over. It's like in her mind the *Dr. Mario* pieces are falling into place. "You're smart. You're a good writer." She nods knowingly. "*That's* why you're like this."

SKATING RINK

It is true that I don't have any friends.

But it is also true that something always happens at the skating rink. I become someone different. For one night, I become someone who could be someone's friend.

Tonight is the skating party at the 49th Street Galleria. Short Angie arranged it, and I am only invited because everyone in the Gifted and Talented class is invited. So Johanna is here, like I knew she would be. Johanna.

We used to go skating together, sometimes. I, of course, have never been able to skate, but this is the early nineties, and there are only so many places for birthday parties, so we went to the skating rink. I love the skating rink. I love the smell of plasticky nacho cheese and pizza with cheap sauce and antiseptic spray behind the rental counter, where the skates I get are always too big or too small no matter what size I ask for.

And Johanna. She would laugh as I put one foot in front of the other, because if you've never seen someone with an undiagnosed cerebellar astrocytoma skate, there's a good reason for it. I'd exaggerate each clunky move, pretending to fall at every turn, making fun of myself before someone else could. That was how I did a lot of things, before the accident. Now I don't have that luxury. Now, if I make fun of myself, people just look at me, pity me. Now everyone in Gifted and Talented knows why I can't skate.

And now I have no Johanna.

I wear a new outfit to the party. It includes a white shirt, three-quarter sleeve, with a name brand across the front in puffy green letters. It also includes a green plaid skirt I didn't know was hideous until I got here, and skin-tight leggings I kind of suspected were hideous but bought anyway, because what if I fall? My ears are pierced now, and even though they make my head hurt, I wear dangly earrings.

There's a line to rent skates, so I stand behind the other people who don't have their own Rollerblades. Everyone else is wearing a T-shirt and shorts. I don't just look overdressed, I look literally *over dressed*—they're all wearing about a third less clothing than I am. I sit on a bench and lace up my skates. They are too tight.

Not to say the skating rink has lost its magic entirely. There's still the disco-ball snowing flakes of light onto the marred, dull swimming-pool blue of the rink. There's still

Top 40 music blaring from the speakers, making me feel cooler just by hearing it.

I hang over the half wall separating the rink from the rest of the world and watch as everyone else skates onto the blue. They stop, polite, when they see me, because they are the smart, courteous Gifted and Talented kids. Some of them ask, "Are you going to come out?"

I say maybe later, although technically I'm not supposed to skate at all—not without a helmet. I shouldn't be here, what with the no helmet and the inability to skate anyway and the leggings and what was I thinking?

Johanna. I watch Johanna skate past with her new best friend, Natalie, who used to be best friends with Lisa, but everyone knows elementary-school best friends don't last, not in junior high. Besides, Lisa is skating with Dallin and Tall Angie, her new best friends, and I know she isn't noticing Natalie laughing with Johanna, and she isn't thinking how she used to be the one making Natalie laugh like that. No, she is not.

She is doing what she is supposed to be doing, which is moving on, which is making friends, which is fitting in and letting go, and they all get in a long line and they speed up and make a whip. In my mind, I slow it down, watch them frame by frame, and they are perfect and laughing and in one long, single line, and I am watching from the half wall, because I can't skate and, even if I could, I'm not supposed to. Not without a helmet.

"Hey, can I ask you something?"

I haven't noticed her come over or stand next to me,

even though I should have because she couldn't have glided over—she's still on the carpet, like I am. You can't creep up on someone when you're wearing skates on carpet.

The girl has long black hair—waist-length—silver hoops, a crop top, and short-shorts showing off perfect, caramel-colored skin. In contrast, you can't even *see* any of my skin, my earrings are trying-too-hard dangly peace signs, and my pixie cut isn't even pixie-cut long over the scar on the back of my head.

I have a feeling I'm setting myself up by letting her ask me something, but I can't think how to say no, so I nod.

"Will you . . ." She looks me in the eye, pleads with me. "Will you hang out with me tonight?"

And, as always, something happens at the skating rink. I become someone different. For one night, I become someone who could be someone's friend.

In fourth grade, it was Yoriko. I met her at a cast party after I played Miss Hannigan in a production of *Annie*. Yoriko played Grace, the assistant to Daddy Warbucks, and she was tall and elegant and nothing like me, and we were double-cast so I only saw her at performances if my Grace couldn't be there. But then, that night she skated up to me like we were old friends. She pulled me along while she skated, and when people joked about it, she only skated faster and never let me fall. And when she asked, "Do you want to be friends?" I was so stunned I didn't even answer her.

And tonight, tonight it is Malia, Malia who asks: "Will you hang out with me? Will you act like we're friends?"

She is beautiful and trendy and nothing like me, but I know exactly how she feels. Tonight, I don't waste any time before saying yes. "Let's laugh," I say, and she doesn't waste any time before laughing with me. I laugh with her like she is the one I want to be laughing with, and so does she.

REMBRANDT'S LAST LETTER

DEAR JOHANNA,
I HAVE BEEN WAY STRESSED FINISHING UP THIS
SEMESTER B/C ALL MY TEACHERS HAVE BEEN
PILING ON PROJECTS AND TESTS LIKE YOU WOULD
NOT BELIEVE. I THINK IT IS ONLY GOING TO GET
WORSE.

SO I'VE BEEN THINKING AND HERE'S THE THING.
I AM SUPER BUSY NOW AND YOU SAY YOU ARE
SUPER BUSY NOW AND IT IS GETTING HARDER TO
FIND TIME TO WRITE, ESPECIALLY B/C I MADE THE
TENNIS TEAM AND THE SEASON STARTS SOON
AND MY BACKHAND IS KINDA WEAK AND WILL
NEED TONS OF PRACTICE.

THE OTHER THING IS COMPLICATED, BUT MY
FRIENDSHIP WITH EM IS STARTING TO CHANGE.
KINDA LIKE HOW YOUR FRIENDSHIP WITH HER
STARTED TO CHANGE LAST YEAR AND NOW
YOU AREN'T FRIENDS AT ALL, B/C THAT'S WHAT
HAPPENS SOMETIMES?

WELL, WHEN HER AND MY FRIENDSHIP STARTED
TO CHANGE I REALIZED I THINK I LIKE HER AS
MORE THAN A FRIEND. AND I THINK THAT COULD
BE GOOD B/C I THINK SHE MAYBE FEELS THE SAME.
MAYBE. BUT I KNOW I WANT TO FIND OUT.

WHAT WE HAVE IS A REAL, SOLID FRIENDSHIP
THAT HAS LASTED FOR YEARS, AND I THINK WE'RE
BOTH READY TO TAKE IT TO THE NEXT LEVEL. SO
TO DO THAT, AND TO REALLY MOVE ON WITH HER,
I NEED TO STOP WRITING TO YOU.

I THINK YOU UNDERSTAND B/C IT SOUNDS LIKE
YOU ARE BUSY TOO AND MAKING NEW FRIENDS
AND EVEN PROBABLY FINDING A GUY YOU LIKE. SO
GOOD LUCK, JOHANNA. REALLY. GOOD LUCK. YOU
WILL ALWAYS BE SPECIAL TO ME.

PEACE.

REMBRANDT

The Thank-God-She-Got-Hit-By-A-Car Girl.
Maybe I am all better *now*?

HOW IT DOESN'T HAPPEN

Here is how it doesn't happen: My hair doesn't quickly grow back into a shiny, cute, regular-teen-girl mane. My headaches don't gradually get better until they disappear entirely. When I go to physical therapy, I don't get stronger and stronger and watch my right hand become functional because the only thing holding it back was the brain tumor and now that it's gone I'm healed and hunky-dory. I don't start playing sports. My tumor-free body doesn't prove that deep within me has always lived a tennis star waiting to be set free.

With time, I don't go back to reading as fast as I used to before the accident. Homework doesn't get easier. I don't find friends who really *get* me, who support me through thick and thin. I do not get less anxious. I do not get less sad. I do not feel like the Thank-God-She-Got-Hit-By-A-Car Girl.

What happens is this: By eighth grade, I can read more and more without getting headaches, but it takes me longer to finish books. I get a free period for homework. I become editor of my junior high school newspaper. I keep writing. My headaches are worse than they've ever been, and doctors can't tell me why, exactly, just that head injuries are different for everyone. The woozy-headed feeling doesn't go away, and I start calling it Wooze-Head, and it becomes my constant companion. I go to physical therapy, and before long, my arms and legs work, and to look at me you'd never know I was hit by a car.

The angular scar on my forehead fades a little bit every day, and I rub it with vitamin E oil like I'm supposed to, and by the time ninth grade rolls around, you can't see it unless you look close. I still don't use Bad Hand. I still have a doctor's note getting me out of PE. I take a full college-prep load, so I don't have time for a free period, but I manage good grades without it. Most medicines don't work. I shorten Wooze-Head to Woo-Head, and the nickname fits, so it sticks. I am lonely and overwhelmed most of the time. I keep writing.

In tenth grade I start Midvalley High School. I sleep a lot. I get a bicycle, and I practice until I can ride it well enough not to get made fun of. I wear a helmet. The neuropsychologist recommends I get a part-time job to "provide me with increased independence and self-esteem." So I bus tables at the ice-cream parlor next to Payless ShoeSource, and every day I go to work and cross the street where I got hit by a car. I keep writing. One of my English assignments gets published in the school paper, and I'm chosen to be on the newspaper staff, even though I'm only a sophomore. My parents announce we are moving to New Galilee.

When people find out my story, they're always amazed. They call me the Thank-God-She-Got-Hit-By-A-Car Girl.

Dear Mr. and Mrs. Wing,

I appreciated your willingness to participate
in the follow-up study of adolescents who have
sustained head injuries. I enjoyed providing a
neuropsychological evaluation for Emily and
meeting with you to discuss the results.

Since her evaluation three years ago, Emily at
sixteen has made positive gains in cognitive
functioning. Her full-scale IQ has increased by
a standard deviation. Consistent with previous
testing, Emily continues to have difficulty
with tasks involving motor skills and is better
at verbal tasks. She excels at understanding
and using language. Particularly, Emily's
written skills have remained superior. Emily
is motivated to succeed and works hard to
achieve that success.

One of the concerns you expressed was
Emily's high level of anxiety. Anxiety and
depression, however, were noted before the
head injury. Emily's anxiety and obsessiveness
are definitely problems for her, and I think
she tends to minimize these problems. Emily

is cognizant of the progress she has made, and I think has a hard time seeing herself as anything but improved from the days in seventh grade (obviously a very tough time for her). She seemed determined to portray herself as "all better."

This, however, does not mean that her anxiety, obsessive and ruminative tendencies, and depression are not interfering with her making further progress. It was quite clear from the very simple Incomplete Sentences form she filled out today that her worries are excessive.

Emily also reports feeling angry, which is frustrating for her. You have noted an increase in her aggressive behavior, and Emily reports this is due to her anger. This behavior is likely also a manifestation of her high anxiety level.

I suggest that Emily be evaluated for possible medication therapy. I hate to see her feeling so tense and anxious if medications could relieve some of this. I certainly think it is worth a consult with a child/adolescent psychiatrist.

What Emily needs now are treatments, not further assessments. I recognize that you are a very busy family, but I also know you care deeply for Emily and want to do whatever is needed to help her. Please let me know if you have any questions or if I can help you in any other way.

Sincerely,
Cecil Che Chen, PhD
Professor and Licensed Psychologist

WRINKLED PANTS

New Doctor is wearing wrinkled pants. Again.

It's not like I'm one to talk. I've never successfully ironed anything in all my seventeen years. Ironing is so awkward. No matter how many times I watch someone else and try to copy their motions, I end up pulling when I'm supposed to push and getting the cord stuck under my wrist. Ironing is, like everything, easier for right-handers.

But at least I know better than to wear the kind of pants that will look like a crumpled grocery bag by four in the afternoon. C'mon, Doc. Buy a cotton-poly blend.

I can't hold a therapist the way some people can't hold a job. One of us always gets frustrated and moves on. *This just isn't working out.*

New Doctor was a recommendation from another doctor. They think I don't realize they're passing me off, but how can I not? I'd do the same thing, if I could.

Usually I go into therapy appointments alone. We talk about everything that's wrong with me on the inside, and it never makes anything less wrong. Afterward my mom goes in and talks to the therapist while I wait on the sofa. The sofa is always blue. I read back issues of *Highlights* and *Parents* and *Newsweek* and pretend not to care what they are saying about me.

But New Doctor is different because we don't talk at all. He gives me pills and asks me yes-or-no questions and gets mad if I say anything else. And he makes my mom come with me. It's yet another part of me that's lamer than lame: I'm a high school junior who only uses mind-altering drugs under adult supervision.

I've been to enough doctors' offices that I now judge them on a multipoint rubric, and New Doctor fails on all counts. His walls are blank except for diplomas in over-sized mattes and thick frames, which is fine, because I like to check up on my health-care professionals. Hofstra undergrad, docs from University of Iowa. Passable. I don't mind stark walls—blank space is better than some hideous pastel landscape that looks like it was stolen from a Holiday Inn.

What I don't like are doctor's offices that don't even *pretend* to look like doctor's offices. The room's got no token object to represent he's an MD—no scale, no stethoscope, no blood-pressure cuff. And the PhDs at least have tissues, and plants, and a wall clock. New Doctor just looks like a lawyer who hasn't finished moving offices yet.

I don't trust him.

"Okay, so . . ." He looks at his clipboard before saying my name. "Emily.

"We started you on . . . Luvox last time. How is that working out?"

It isn't. I'm no better than I was before the medication. Still anxious and unhappy. Still Woo-Head. Still the not-right, weird, backward girl with a Bad Hand. Oh, and since I've moved to New Galilee earlier this year, I have a whole new set of reasons why pills will never be enough to fix me.

New Doctor nods at me. It looks like he's trying to head-butt me with his imaginary set of antlers, but I guess it's a nonverbal cue to get me to talk.

"Luvox makes me tired," I tell him. I try not to look at his pants.

"But is it helping?"

I pause before answering, because this is the kind of question that could be a trick. These kind of doctors sometimes act like they understand you to your face, but then they scribble down something totally different, something random, like you exhibit signs of aggression because you mentioned your fingers tingling. Must proceed with caution.

"It helps me sleep." This isn't as sarcastic as it sounds, not if you know me. I've never been good at falling asleep, even when I was a baby, from what I've heard. It's not the sleepiness I mind—it's the sleepiness all the time, an exhaustion so thick it's painful to hold my head up.

"Drowsiness is common at first. It can get better."

When something *can* get better, it never applies to me.

New Doctor takes a note. Or at least pretends to. He is right-handed. "I'm going to change the dose."

Change the dose. I know what that means. It means he doesn't want to try anything else. He's already given up on me, the way so many before him have. The way I've given up on him.

New Doctor works at the university, so we've parked underground. It's cold and the van is far away. "I'll drive, okay?" my mom says.

She knows I'll agree with her. She knows I'm not a normal teenager, the kind who wants to drive, the kind who has a license, or is eager to get one. I'm not the kind of teenager who can drive without thinking about what could happen. What could go wrong.

"I think there's a Smith's near here. I need to get hamburger buns while we're out."

"Fine." It's not dinnertime yet, but it looks like it is. I hate this time of year. The early darkness makes me feel like I'm late for something all the time.

My mom never gets cold. Her Alaska-bred body is hearty like that. I'm shivering, and she's not even wearing a coat. "You know, you weren't exactly working with him in there."

"I was trying," I say. This is only half to two-thirds true. At first, after the accident, I tried to work with them. More than that. I tried to please them. I tried to have a good attitude. I tried be jovial and not act like I was sleepy or antsy from the waiting and the not-knowing. I tried to answer how they wanted me to answer and take what they wanted me to take and keep track of what they wanted me to keep track of.

Now I'm tired. Every promise of healing is shallow—a pool with only three feet of cures. Anyone who has to swim deeper for answers can only bump their head against the aquamarine concrete again and again. I'm tired of bumping. It only makes my head bleed.

Mom unlocks both minivan doors. I hit my shoes against the side before getting in so the snow shakes off. The heater hums. There's no music. She stops to make a left-hand turn, but the cars come steady in both directions, as consistent as a string of red-and-white Christmas lights, so we wait.

"Honestly, Emily," she says. "Sometimes I think you don't even want to get better."

I don't answer. Maybe this is half to two-thirds true, too. Maybe I *don't* want to get better. Every time I get close to getting better, something worse happens.

When it comes to me, even bad luck has a price.

SHRINKS I HAVE KNOWN

Marsha

Dr. John

Pregnant Jill and the lady with the flower scar

Dr. Cohen, who gave me the test to graduate from
The Children's Center

Mrs. Leed, the elementary school counselor

Dr. John again

Darcy, child life specialist (helping patients cope
with hospital stressors)

Dr. Kern, psychologist

Dr. Hendler, child psychiatrist

Social worker who gave me the creepy
teddy bear with teeth

Dr. Halestrom, neuropsychologist

Dr. Chen, educational psychologist

New Doctor

CARNIVAL OF LIFE

Nobody here is supposed to know about the accident.
In New Galilee, I am no longer the Thank-God-She-Got-Hit-By-A-Car Girl. And my mom—she is no longer that girl's mother.

It's an unspoken promise I made to her when she first talked about us moving. We were driving, turning our minivan at the corner where it all happened. She said, "I can't believe I still live on this street. How can I still live on this street?" Her freckles turned pink, this funny thing they did whenever she was sad or mad.

This time I think it was both, because there were tears in her eyes and her voice, but there were also clenched hands on the steering wheel and a silence so loud I could only hear the *clickity-clickity-clickity* of the blinker. And that night there were a bunch of info sheets on the counter next to the phone, advertising houses that were Spacious and Immaculate and Not On This Street.

So I'm surprised when someone here knows about me. Not a seventeen-year-old someone, either—a Mom's-age someone. I'm at a church carnival.

The thing about the Church is, it's the same everywhere you go. The layout is the same in basically every building: a big chapel in the front, a Cultural Hall/gym behind that, a Primary room for the kids in one corner, and a Relief Society room for the women in another corner. Same polished chrome trays for the sacrament, same lettering on the outside wall: THE CHURCH OF JESUS CHRIST OF LATTER-DAY SAINTS. VISITORS WELCOME. So whether you're in Southeastville, Virginia, or New Galilee, Utah, you know what you're in for.

I like this, partly because order comforts me, but mostly because the brick-and-mortar buildings remind me of my faith: the same no matter where I am.

The Church as an organization doesn't always remind me of my faith. The Church as an organization reminds me of The Man.

In the Church, everywhere you go, the teens ages twelve through eighteen meet on a weekday night. Usually we divide up into smaller groups, and I'm with the other young women ages sixteen through eighteen. But once a month, all the teenagers combine for an activity. That's what tonight is.

Tonight's carnival is not a real carnival, with a Ferris wheel and churros. It pretends to be a real carnival. I mean, they don't try that hard because, you know, no churros. But the church gym is decorated with helium balloons and tiny lights, and they do have glazed doughnuts.

You get a certain number of tokens, and then, if you go to the good-choice booths, you get white tickets and, if you go to the bad-choice booths, you get red tickets. It's pretty obvious that the carnival is supposed to be like life, because the bad-choice booths are carnival-ish, with games like ringtoss and basketball free throw and golf putting. The good-choice games aren't even games—Name That Hymn, Scripture Chase, Serve the Old Guy.

Part of me feels like this is wrong on so many levels that I don't know where to start. But a bigger part of me can tell the leaders put a bunch of time into this, and boycotting seems just plain mean. I want to be a team player, although I know Team Adult is probably not the team I should be joining.

One booth is a fortune-teller. It's just Sister Fawson with a scarf over her head and a round light fixture as a crystal ball. She waves her fingers, takes turns between looking at me and looking into the ball. "I sense that you are new in this town," she says with a thick accent from Nowhereland.

"That's right!" I say, to play along, even though this is my present—not much of a fortune.

"I see you are very smart." She looks at me and smiles. "You take many advanced classes at school. It will serve you well." The fortune-teller tent is one of the bad-choice booths, but this is church, so even when you're making bad life decisions, it's hard to avoid moralizing.

"And you have had a difficult past." Her eyes cloud over. "Yes, yes, I see many trials. You were in . . . an accident, yes?"

This I wasn't expecting. But I nod.

"You have suffered much. But you have also learned much. And I see that this will serve you well. You have endured. You have overcome." She takes her hands off the ball. When she speaks, her accent is gone. "Because you're okay now, right?" It's a request. "Now you're all better?"

HIDING AT CHURCH

Here I am. At church in New Galilee. But I feel better when I'm not actually *in* church.

I feel better when I'm in my family's beat-up Dodge Caravan. It smells like sour milk. The heat makes it worse. Still, I sit sidesaddle in the passenger seat, legs sprawled beneath the steering wheel. Not a great position for a girl in tights, skirt hiked up.

Even this existence is preferable to Sunday school with the dewy-faced, golden-haired idiots who I have to hang out with just because they happen to be my age.

Every Sunday they talk about what they did the night before. Every Sunday they were together the night before. I don't care, I don't want to spend my Saturday nights with them anyway, recapping soccer games and playing laser tag and watching cheesy old movies like *E.T.* But then Sunday school starts, and they stop talking and look bored, and they dare me to act interested. And honestly, class isn't that interesting, but it's better than listening to their social calendar. So now I skip all of it, and I read Scriptures in the minivan, and when I get tired of that, I think about what God looks like, and what I'd ask Him if I knew He'd answer every question.

I think: *How is it possible to alternately hate and love my religion with such passion on each side?*

I think: *How is it possible only to feel close to God when I'm viewing His house from the rearview mirror?*

DEBATE TOURNAMENT

I know it has to stop.

I am way too old when I realize it. Junior year. Debate trip. It's a two-day tournament in Logan, a town far enough away that we stay overnight. The bus picks us up from school early on Friday, right after lunch. The only chaperone is Bill, our "coach"—an old guy who seems to care more about where we're going to eat dinner than anything else. It's a breeding ground for mayhem, and this fact has not escaped us.

We shuffle onto the bus. We're a ragtag team. There's Char, semi-Goth. Hair striped black and magenta, nose ring, dark lipstick. Political. Smart. Obsessed with sex, but that might be just for show. At tournaments, she dresses like a banker, complete with sensible shoes. She takes it seriously.

The Sara(h)s. They don't take it seriously. Sarah-with-*h* is an actress who does humorous interp. She's memorized one monologue, a comic spin on *Romeo and Juliet,* and then she's out. Sara-no-*h* doesn't even have an event. She just sort of does whatever and it works. That's how everything goes for Sara-no-*h*.

Hansen and Clark. They've been a duo since seventh grade. They carry a briefcase—just one, between them. It has a lucky Transformer inside that has a long story behind it, but I guess you had to be there because it makes no sense to the rest of us.

Hansen and Clark are policy debaters, and they're good. Everyone wants to be them. Even if you don't care about policy debate, even if you don't care about debate in general, watching them in action is so beautiful it makes you *wish* you cared about debate. Makes you wish you could do that, too—speak with such speed and agility, persuading with reason and rhetoric.

Hansen looks like a little boy—a cute little boy, with sticky-out ears and neatly combed hair, but still a little boy. He has this annoying voice that becomes endearing with time. Clark is brilliant. He's always using words no one else has heard of, or old, dated expressions no one else has heard of, either. He has this feathered brown hair like a seventies actor, so of course I like him. Of course no one's supposed to know. And of course everyone does.

My being on the debate team is a mystery to everyone, including me. I don't like debate. I'm naturally competitive, but it's not a trait I like about myself. Before each round, it's like my brain is being vacuumed out and replaced by a balloon filled with panic. Fight or flight. I hate choosing fight because bad things have always happened when I've chosen it in the past. But in debate when you choose flight, you lose.

I'm on the debate team for my dad. My dad is like me: There are many things he can't do, but what he can do, he does very, very well. One of his things is debate—he was a star in high school and college. My thing is writing. At my old school, I wrote for the newspaper. At this school, I can't, because the staff was chosen before I moved here—invitation-only.

Everything about this place is invitation-only.

Everything except the debate team.

When my dad saw how I had no real writing here and no real friends here, he swept in the best way he knew how: I joined the debate team, and he became our de facto coach. He's great at it, but it wouldn't matter even if he weren't. It doesn't take a superstar to be better than Bill.

So here I am, on the debate team bus with my new "friends," my complete terror of debate, and Bill asleep on the front bench.

I've got a window seat, and Char is sitting next to me in a pin-striped pencil skirt. The Sara(h)s are in front of us, turned backward on the bench, laughing at a joke I forgot to listen to. This is a good moment, a happy-girl moment. If a movie camera has been following me around since I moved to New Galilee, this is the happiest scene it's caught on tape, bar none. I should feel happy.

I never feel the way I should.

I look across and two rows over at Clark, who is laughing with Hansen, and I feel better. Better than I should, considering that Clark is not my boyfriend, or even my friend, when you get right down to it. Why should seeing him make me smile? But it does.

Char sees it, of course, and follows my gaze and nods. "He knows you like him."

Geez. This is like every bad teen movie ever made.

I look away from her, out the window. We're heading into a canyon. White letters on a green sign say: RUN-AWAY TRUCK RAMP 1 MILE. "He does not."

"He does. Hansen told him."

"Hansen doesn't know." That's a lie, because Hansen does know. I told him during a moment of vulnerability at a tournament last month, when we were partners because Clark plays the bass and had an orchestra concert.

We were connecting, sort of, and it was the first time I'd connected with anyone since moving to this place. He asked me why I was on the debate team since it was clear I didn't want to be, and I told him about my dad and my no friends and how it made as much sense as anything else, and he told me how his mom liked his brother better than she liked him and how he wanted to sing in Madrigals but was scared he wouldn't make it.

It was the closest I'd felt to friendship in a long time, and it was with this kid with pokey-out ears and a Transformer that he kept rubbing with his thumb. And he was Clark's best friend, so I said, "Does he have a girlfriend?" And Hansen knew I wasn't talking about the Transformer.

Hansen said "Why, do you like him?" and I nodded and Hansen shook his head and said: "Don't. If you like Clark, your life is gonna suck. Clark doesn't have time to get involved with high school girls. Clark and me, we want no part of it."

And I nodded and said okay and made him promise not to say anything to Clark.

But he did.

He did, and now Clark knows, and it will be awkward and now we'll never even be friends, and I will never have friends here, I will be on this team fighting stupid debate fights that aren't even real, and I can't lose or my dad will be sad, and I can't make him sad again, not after crushing Maude. I stare out the window and tell myself to stay calm, to focus, to think: RUNAWAY TRUCK RAMP 1 MILE.

"Hansen told Clark," Char says, "that you want to be his *girlfriend*."

No one is safe. Nowhere I go. Because no one means it when they're nice to you, and no one means what they say and RUNAWAY TRUCK RAMP. RUNAWAY TRUCK RAMP.

But I can't do it anymore, and I nudge Char out of her seat and scoot through the aisle. I bump into a few benches on the way because we're moving and my coordination is what it is already. There will be bruises. Char and the Sara(h)s are following me, and that fiery balloon of panic is where my broken brain should be.

There is no brain left, not even a broken one, when I get to Hansen and Clark. Hansen is in the aisle seat and he looks up at me and smiles a smug, pretty-boy smile, a taunt or a leer more than a smile. There is a biology textbook resting between them.

I do not look at Clark when I grab the book tight in two hands. My right fist shakes. Everything shakes. "Seriously, Tyler?" I use his first name. I hope it hurts. "Seriously?"

And the book comes crashing down on his head. I imagine it being beautiful, magnificent, final. But the bus is going too fast and I hit too hard and everyone is silent when it thunks. It's not a comic-book, lighthearted thunk, but a painful, scary, concussion-style thunk. I feel the eyes on me. I hear the whispers that haven't started yet.

Char is horrified. "I was kidding," she says weakly. "He didn't really say that."

Hansen is gently touching his head, his Transformer splayed on the floor. There's an expression on his face I've never seen before. I've seen him mad plenty of times. In debate, it's your job to get mad. But this is different; this is anger. "What is *wrong* with you?" he asks.

My eyes go big, vacant, scared. My knees give out and I don't know how to answer him. So I am on the floor with the broken Transformer, everything that is wrong with me fighting for center stage in the place where my brain should be. All I can say is *I'm sorry. I'm so, so sorry.*

And I know this has to stop. This part that's wrong with me—the out-of-control anger, the out-of-control violence—it ends now.

DADDY

Dad's lying down again when I come home from my church activity. He is sprawled across his bed, looks of subtle anguish flashing across his face as quick as the lightning beating on the window. I know his shoulder is bothering him again. It always is, lately.

I hate my parents' bedroom. It still has the southwestern-style wallpaper the previous owners put up, swirls of turquoise and pink and Day-Glo orange. Not my mother's style at all, or mine. Honestly, it shouldn't be anyone's. The wallpaper is just another reminder how wrong this is; how much we don't fit here. Especially me.

Their room is right across the hall from mine, so it's easy to check in with Dad before I retreat from the rest of the house. I sit next to him, in the triangle of space between his feet and the edge of the mattress. "It's your shoulder again." Which goes without saying. "Do you know what's wrong yet, Dad?"

"Just the meanness in me coming out," he says. Then, when I look puzzled: "My father always used to say that when I was in pain. It was just my meanness coming out."

You know that moment when you are so overcome with love for someone you never want to cause them any more pain, ever again? And you cry because you know you will? That is the moment I'm in right now.

Grandpa didn't die until I was thirteen, but I didn't know him even when he was alive. By the time I was born, his disease had shut him out of my world entirely. We'd go to visit him at the nursing home sometimes, but he talked slow and garbled, and the kids were excused early. I'd go in the hallway, where the floors were shiny, and play a game where I could only step on the reflections from the fluorescent light beams overhead, and the punishment for missing one was that I had to stay in this place forever, with its peculiar smell that made my head hurt and its residents who wore booties.

Much later, I learned about him in bits and pieces. Nobody wanted to talk about it, but Grandpa was what used to be called manic-depressive. When he wasn't well, which was often, he'd hurt the people closest to him—the people who later became closest to *me*.

Meanness came out all over the place in my father's father.

I wonder if I'm like him. Not Dad—I know I'm like him. We have the same sense of humor and drive, and we're the same kind of clumsy. But Grandpa.

They call manic-depression *bipolar disorder* now, and in AP Psychology, I've copied down notes, and sometimes I think it sounds exactly like me. Because most of the time there's this darkness inside I can't explain, and then some nights I'll start writing and the words come so easy and so right and I'm so happy, and before I know it, the light is shining through the slats in the blinds and it's morning already. Maybe I have bipolar disorder, too. Maybe drugs don't work for me the same way they didn't work for Grandpa.

I think Dad sees my tears because he changes the subject and says, "I typed up your English paper. It's on the computer now, so you can look it over before printing it."

I type about sixteen WPM because of Bad Hand. No matter how many typing classes I take, my right hand just crumples over *jkl*, completely useless. Usually it seems as if Dad likes to type for me—he goes fast, and sometimes I sit next to him and watch his hands fly over the keys. But today: "Dad, your shoulder. You didn't have to do that, really."

"It only took a few minutes," he says, and that's the end of it, so I say thank you.

He's quiet for a minute. He closes his eyes. "It's good," he says. "Your writing. It's very, very good. You have talent, Em. Follow your dream." He pauses again. I can't tell if it's from the pain. "Don't make the same mistake I did."

"In the backward world that is Hollins, that's the first time this backward girl has finally fit."

HOLLINS

"Excuse me, are you going to Hollins?" I'm in the Atlanta International Airport, waiting for a connecting flight to Roanoke, Virginia, the first time I see her. The girl's skin is colorful and shimmering, like the face of an Egyptian princess. Her tie-dyed shirt hangs loose on her ample chest; dozens of silver rings stack like pancakes on her fingers.

I nod. I nod partly because yes, I am going to Hollins, and partly with admiration. What if I *wasn't* going to Hollins? What if I didn't know what, or where, or who Hollins was? She would look the fool, but she's willing to risk it. I like that, and I'm not used to it—someone else taking the initiative; someone else willing to look the fool. Already, I can tell this will be a through-the-looking-glass experience. Completely backward of everything I thought I knew.

Dani takes quick stock of me: long, well-groomed brown hair; soft-yellow Ralph Lauren polo shirt I bought at Ross Dress for Less with my grandma; khaki skirt. She extends her hand anyway. "I'm Dani."

Daniela Elise Davenport comes from old money, is oddly fixated on Plath and Poe, and has aspirations to go to Smith. She's going to the Hollins high school program because she loves creative writing, loves women's colleges, and can't stand to spend the summer at home with her mother.

She doesn't ask why I'm going to Hollins—maybe she knows that my reasons are the same.

I've wanted to go to Hollins ever since I flipped through a college guide and saw that the author of *Goodnight Moon* was an alumna. The moment I wrote my first installment of The Medallions, I knew I wanted to write for kids and teens for the rest of my life. Hollins treats that like a legitimate academic course.

Besides, Hollins is this secluded, idyllic campus with ivy-covered buildings and big trees and lots of history, where women ride on horseback to the nearby creek. I'm allergic to horses, but still—when I find out about the high school writing program, I want to go more than I've wanted anything in my life.

That said, my first night at Hollins is terrifying. Our flight is late, and by the time we arrive, the dining hall is closed. The vending machine has only caffeinated soda, the kind my mom doesn't allow for religious reasons, and the drinking fountain in the dorm is jammed. I'm more thirsty than I am hungry, and I'm pretty hungry.

I drink from a faucet in the third-floor bathroom. The girls getting ready for bed spread on their creams and foam up their gels and pretend not to look at me. I try to call my parents from a pay phone in the hall, using the number from a calling card they gave me to cover long-distance charges. I succeed only in reaching, and I am dead serious, "America's Hottest Sex Line."

My roommate, Carrie, is on her bed—her tanned legs bent at the knee, her feet waving back and forth, conducting imaginary music in the stifling, humid air. Her bed has the same white coverlet that mine will have, once I make it. But I have no energy for something as pedestrian as making my bed. Right now my linens just wait there, rolled up neatly, like a pill.

I slip out of my shoes and lie on the disgusting blue-and-white-striped mattress, facedown, past the point of caring what's been on that mattress before me. I thump my head against the bedroll like I used to thump my head against my pillow when I was a little girl. Back then, the pain made the other pain not hurt so much. This time it just makes the pain three-dimensional. My stomach growls.

Carrie's been reading *Allure*, and I hear her set it down. "Here," she says, handing me a foil-wrapped cereal bar, one with fruit filling. "This should help. Oh, and you didn't miss out on anything tonight. Dinner sucked."

Besides being a writer, everybody here is something. Lauren's a clarinet player from Long Island. Rachael is a street artist with a do-rag. Valerie's a hippie. Katherine's a flamenco dancer. Leann's a photographer. Erica's designing her own line of furniture. Courtney is rich.

And me—I'm not the Thank-God-She-Got-Hit-By-A-Car Girl. For real this time. No one knows because it never comes up. When I lay in the hospital and wondered if I could ever go a day without thinking about it, without talking about it, without dealing with it? That day has arrived. It's so subtle I don't notice. I don't realize I'm not the Head Case until I see what I *am* besides being a writer. I am a Mormon.

Some people live their whole lives having their Mormonism make them unique, but this is my first experience with it. Even before I moved to New Galilee, where the LDS membership hovers around 96 percent, I lived in places where my beliefs were common. At breakfast, girls ask me why I don't drink either coffee *or* tea and if I read the Book of Mormon and why they can't go into LDS temples. I answer them quick and confident, like a game-show champion. If there's one thing I know about, it's my religion.

I'm not sure how it happens, how I meet people without trying, but it happens. It's like something that happens to other girls, not to me: I hang out with Carrie, and she hangs out with Valerie, who hangs out with Leann, and we all just kind of fit together.

Carrie is from Virginia Beach, so she drove here, her car stuffed full. Anything you could need, Carrie has it—an extra pillow, moleskin for a blister, a silk flower to wear for the talent show. Valerie's tiny—elfin, pixie—convinced she has a triangle-shaped head, and paranoid about it. She's fresh off a breakup, so we spend a lot of time cursing the name of a boy we've never met. Leann goes to the computer lab seven times a day to check her e-mail. Afterward, she regales us with tales of her gay best friend and his various suitors.

Before long, we're borrowing the disgusting blue-and-white mattresses from the empty bedroom next door. We order pizza and talk about the weird guys from the Latin camp staying on the third floor, and we sleep four in a row, like it always should have been, like it was at those sleepovers I never had.

EASY AS ABC

In the backward world that is Hollins, making friends is easy, writing is hard.

My creative-writing class starts with writing poetry, and I'm terrible. Poetry has always eluded me—I can't tell the difference between a good poem and a bad one. Details that I know are significant seem insignificant, and I can't hear meter. Our classroom has picture-frame windows looking over the quad, and we sit around a solid walnut table. The other girls are reading their work aloud, and from their polished, sure way of reading, I know their stuff is something to be proud of. I don't deserve Hollins. I don't deserve the beauty around me.

My teacher, an assistant professor named Susannah, soothes me in a voice that is calm, slow, and Southern: "This struggle you're having? It's a sign something good is coming." She looks at me intensely, with deep blue-gray eyes. "That's how it works."

It's the second Wednesday at Hollins. Carrie's still in class, so I'm in my room with Valerie, sitting across from her at an identical desk. She's giving me a quiz on my "Guy-Gettin' Style." I'm half answering, half editing something I wrote for class, and half staring out the window next to me, letting in the humid air that's nothing like what I was used to before but is exactly what I'm used to now.

That's how I feel here. Like a better version of myself, one that's three halves, one that's more than a hundred percent. I know enough to recognize that this moment, right now, is as close to perfect as I'll ever get.

This week in class we've started our short-story unit. Now writing comes easy again, natural as dreaming. Today, before we broke for lunch, Dani handed me back my manuscript we critiqued in class. *This story is you,* she'd written in bold pink pen. *You* was underlined, twice.

"'You and your crew run into a group of guy friends at the movies, including your crush. What do you do?'" Valerie asks.

"Huh?" The scene outside the window has caught my attention again. It's lush and green, greener than any summer I've ever seen. But if I didn't know better, I'd swear it was Halloween. One girl's hair is in a tight French braid under a fancy riding cap, and she's dressed in full Kentucky Derby attire. A group of girls are coming back from the pool, hair wet and dripping, wearing beach towels like sarongs. The Latin camp guys must be doing a play or something, because a bunch of them are standing around in togas and one of them is pushing a wreath onto another one's head. "What are my choices?"

"'(A) Oh-so-casually slide your arms around him during the first tense scene, (B) offer to share your popcorn, (C) sit as far away from him as humanly possible.'"

It takes me a second to remember that back home, in the real world, I don't have a crew or a group of guy friends. But that has nothing to do with my refusal to choose one of the options. "None of the above," I say. "All those answers are horrible." Valerie nods, and I say: "I could write a better quiz than this."

And it's true. I *could* write a better quiz than this. I'm a writer. No matter who else I've been—the sad, left-handed misfit, the Thank-God-She-Got-Hit-By-A-Car Girl, the Head Case—I've always been a writer. I'll always be a writer.

It's late. Dark out, almost cool, and clear. Everybody wants to be outside on a night like tonight. Becca and Rachael are drawing murals with sidewalk chalk. Simone and Katherine and Lauren are by the makeshift clothesline, checking to see if the bras they tie-dyed earlier have dried yet. Dani and Erica are chain-smoking.

Carrie, Valerie, Leann, and I are watching lightning bugs. I'm the only one who hasn't seen them before, because there are no lighting bugs where I'm from. Carrie lies back, Valerie props on one elbow, Leann picks grass, and they talk, but I just watch the fireflies light up, then stop. Light up, stop. I'm mesmerized. My friends, they don't mind.

And I don't know if Dani looks at me first or I look at her first, but we see each other and under the glow from the Tinker Hall porch light and the cigarette, she winks at me.

In the backward world that is Hollins, that's the first time this backward girl has finally fit.

KRISTIN

Kristin was the first friend I made when I could see the future. It was the first week of senior year at the high school where I was supposed to be an outcast, because that's how I felt most comfortable. We sat beside each other in genetics class, and it was when she looked at me like she'd always known me that I fell in love with her.

Later I found out that she had known me—not for always, but for longer than I'd known her. She remembered me from an English class the year before, when I was the new girl, an English class in which I cannot remember ever speaking a word to anyone. But Kristin told me I spoke to her, and I wondered why we hadn't become friends right then, but maybe it was because I couldn't see the future yet.

When senior year started and Kristin looked at me like she knew me, I saw the rest of the year flash in front of my face: Kristin and me flipping through textbooks and typing up term papers; Kristin and me eating pizza and watching *Ferris Bueller's Day Off*; Kristin and me driving through the empty New Galilee streets at night, the radio up and the windows down. I could even hear the music—Sheryl Crow. It was strangely, startlingly specific.

But the stranger, more startling part is that it all came true. Every last flash of it.

"By October of my senior year, I have friends. Real friends."

MONTAGE

I'm not sure how it happens, how I meet people without trying, but it happens. After a lifetime of living in places that do not want me, and after a year of living in a place that I do not want, by October of my senior year, I have friends. Real friends. I hang out with Kristin, who hangs out with Milla, and they hang out with Lindley, and we all just kind of fit together.

Flash: Kristin and me in her old maroon Cadillac D'elegance, with matching velvety maroon interior that you kind of sink into. It gets dark early, so it feels like we're sneaking out any time we go anywhere. The radio doesn't work well, but turning it up too loud seems to help, and when we land on a Sheryl Crow song and she reaches to change it, I say, "What? Leave it there!" Not because I'm a die-hard Sheryl Crow fan, but because it isn't static. Kristin says, "No, ugh, I hate Sheryl Crow; I'd rather listen to static." The only other station we can get is easy listening, some Michael Bolton ballad, a compromise to no one, but we both seem to hate it equally, and each time we hit a bump in the road, we sink deeper into the seats.

Flash: Kristin and Milla and me at my house, in the office. It's littered with my brother's LEGOs and my mom's paperwork, but out of all of us, my family has the best computer, so here we are. It's the night before our AP English essays are due, and Kristin's typing her paper and I'm at our old, demoted dining room table writing mine longhand. Kristin will type for me because she *clickity-clacks* at the speed of light. Milla's eating fudge my dad made, and she's composed a little ditty about how she loves Dad's fudge and it gets you out of a drudge. It's catchy, but I still throw a copy of *The Grapes of Wrath* at her head because I'm trying to work. She says, "Ow!" I know it didn't really hurt (it's just a paperback), but I apologize anyway because I'm working so hard to be better about hitting people with books, about hitting people with anything, about hitting people in general. And Milla forgives me, and Kristin asks for my paper, and I hand her my first page and she *clickity-clacks*, fingers dancing like a concert pianist.

Flash: Kristin's surprise birthday party, loosely themed around the 1980s so we can reminisce about/make fun of eighties cinema. We start with *Ferris Bueller's Day Off*, because I've never seen it and everyone says that's a travesty. When the pizzas arrive, I pick the pepperoni off my slice because I only like pepperoni essence, and I give the pepperoni disks to Kristin. Lindley falls asleep during *Pretty in Pink*. We don't notice until she starts mumbling, asking us where we put the tools and why we stole her grandma's bras. And then Milla falls asleep, too, so we turn off the movie.

Kristin and I talk about the future, about college. We pull out our catalogs from under the couch, because it's senior year, and college catalogs are always at our fingertips. Kristin says she thinks she'll go to Brigham Young University. She opens up her fat book of general information, and I look through the skinnier list of class offerings, not really paying attention to what I'm reading.

"It's a cliché," I say. "Ninety-six percent of our senior class will apply to BYU. Every Mormon in the country wants to go to BYU."

We both know it's not true, especially for the Mormon University of Utah fans, who hate BYU with a passion. But for the sake of argument, Kristin says: "It might be a cliché, but it's a good school."

"Yes." Out of curiosity, I turn to the list of English courses. And then. Then I see it. *ENGL 310: Writing for Children and Adolescents. Instructor: Plummer, Louise.*

Louise Plummer. *My* Louise Plummer, who writes books like I want to write, who signed my book in sixth grade and wrote to me: *Someday I'll be reading you in print— and I'll be cheering!*

ENGL 310: Writing for Children and Adolescents. Instructor: Plummer, Louise. Prerequisite: ENGL 218 or instructor's consent. I could get instructor consent. I could take a class about writing from a writer I love.

But Hollins. I have to go to Hollins. I push the BYU stuff to the side and show Kristin the glossy Hollins brochure, with the ivy and the brick buildings and the picture-frame windows and the women sitting at a walnut table, engrossed in heated discussion. I tell Kristin about Hollins, about how I want to go there because that's where I fit.

And I'm not sure if she understands, because she looks at me, and she looks at our friends sleeping around us, boxing us in, and she says: "Maybe, but you fit here, too."

YOU WON'T BE SORRY

For me, where I go to college has never been about where I get in; it's about where I get money. I haven't applied to any of the heavy-hitters; even if I get in, I wouldn't want to go there. I want to go to Hollins. Even before I knew about Hollins, I wanted to go to Hollins. Somewhere small and far away, with women both exactly like me and nothing like me. I want four years of last summer: in turns terrifying and overwhelming and magical. And expensive.

So in late April of my senior year, it's coming down to that, to the Benjamins. It's a rare moment of solitude at my house: My brothers are at soccer practice, and my mom is running errands with my little sister, and I have no idea where Juliana is, but whatever—it's quiet.

I'm at the white laminate desk in my room, the one I saved up for in fifth grade and is still hanging on despite the raised bumps like chicken pox from the time I tried to take good care of it but used a too-abrasive cleanser. College miscellanea are spread in front of me. I'm crunching all the numbers, but I know the truth: There's no way I can afford to go to Hollins.

The news that would have devastated me at the beginning of the year now leaves me strangely serene. I'm not numb. I'm not resigned. I'm something else. Last night, my mom said to me, "Dad would never tell you this, but he thinks you should go to BYU. He wants it to be your decision. But he feels, strongly, that you should go to BYU."

I do, too. Feel strongly that I should go to BYU, even though it's never been what I've wanted. I think about taking a class from Louise Plummer and sharing a dorm room with Kristin, and it feels right.

BYU shouldn't feel right. BYU is what feels right to the other people—normal, easygoing, right-handed people. What should feel right to me is Hollins. Where I'd struggle to make ends meet but know I'm being true to my artist's soul. Where I'm far away from everything and everyone I know. Where I might be different, but that's why I fit.

Except there's this voice inside me, and I know it's not my own voice, saying: *You are right wherever you go. You fit. You deserve to have what makes other people happy make you happy.*

And with what I know of life, it surprises me. Because I've never liked icing on cake or brand-new mountain bikes or *E.T.* I've never had the luxury of having what makes other people happy—right-handed people with healthy heads and hearts—make me happy, too.

But God talks to me, and I hear Him. *Give it a try. Go to BYU. You won't be sorry.*

And all I know is that if God's giving me one less thing to be sorry about, I'll take it.

High school graduation ensemble, complete with hat.
This time, the hat makes sense.

THE FINAL GRADUATION DAY

"I need something from you," says Lindley, leaning across the lunch table and looking fake-secretive.

It's my last Spaghetti Day. It's unclear how I fell in love with school spaghetti, because most days I don't eat school lunch, and even if I did I'd get pizza or a sandwich from the Chick-fil-A cart in the student store. Something regular people eat, not the school lunch main entree, which, to my knowledge, not even irregular people eat.

But however I was introduced to school spaghetti, I was hooked, and now I always carry a couple of dollars in my backpack just in case it's Spaghetti Day. And because I graduate in less than a week, this will be my last. I won't miss much about this school, but I will miss that. "Need something like what?" I ask her.

"A picture of you from your childhood."

Kristin sits down next to Lindley, across from me. She has pizza.

"I don't really like to revisit my childhood."

"Did you ask Emily for a picture?" Kristin asks knowingly, opening her chocolate milk.

Lindley rolls her eyes. "It's just a picture. A baby picture. No baggage." She sighs. "Seriously. You need therapy."

I'm always strangely flattered when someone suggests I need therapy. It means they assume I'm not *already* in therapy.

"Hey!" Milla whirls in like a warm wind, on her own time frame, as usual. She sets down her backpack. "What'd I miss?"

Lindley says: "Emily doesn't want to have a past."

"Everybody has a past," says Milla wisely.

She gives it to us the morning of graduation, when the juniors and sophomores are in class, but we're making last-minute preparations. Lindley's a valedictorian and has been practicing her joint speech with Jake, her co-valedictorian. They both have to get to Symphony Hall earlier than the other seniors, but she stops by my house before she leaves. "Happy graduation!" she says, hugging me. She's wearing her new dress, slate blue with a crocheted short-sleeve sweater that matches her eyes.

And seeing her—this smart, beautiful, talented, funny girl, standing on my front porch, holding out a graduation gift to me—it almost brings tears to my eyes. That would be lame, so I don't cry. Trying not to cry has always made me cry, but today it doesn't. Today I take what she's offering.

Lindley's written a poem. I've found a friend who's a writer, and I didn't have to go across the country to find her. She was right here, and she excels at poetry like I never could. Her poem is about all of us, The Crew, and she's framed it in delicate etched silver. In each corner are a set of pictures: baby Kristin and senior Kristin, baby Milla and senior Milla, baby Lindley and senior Lindley, baby Emily and senior Emily.

Baby Emily looks nothing like senior Emily, of course. Baby Emily has no freckles because of the sun and no wound because a normal, middle-aged driver on an only-sort-of-busy-street hit her on a December night. Baby Emily doesn't have a railroad-track incision on the back of her head, or ears that have two holes each because they've been pierced twice but caused her so much pain each time that she let them grow back through. Baby Emily has no scars.

I have all those scars now, but I've never felt more like baby Emily. Like I'm starting over. "Thank you," I tell Lindley. "I love it. I haven't had a friend like you before. Like The Crew."

"Neither have I," she says, this smart, beautiful, talented, funny girl who I'm sure has had plenty of friends like The Crew before.

"I used to have to make up friends," I explain, to make sure she knows the difference. "I made up a best friend. I even made up a boyfriend."

Her eyes light up. "So did I! In junior high. All my friends had boyfriends and I didn't, so I told everyone that I did, that he lived in St. George and I met him on vacation. His name was Trent. I would write him letters."

"Seriously?" And I'm thinking maybe I'm not so backward after all, that maybe all writers are the same, that finally my childhood fits. "Did he write you back?"

Lindsey arches an eyebrow. "Noo." She pauses, then says it slow. "He wasn't real."

There's a split-second of silence and it's perfect. The perfect thing to say, the perfect way to say it, the perfect moment for both of us to realize that maybe I am a little backward, but it's my backward that makes me fit.

And I don't know who starts laughing first, but maybe it's both of us, and we're standing on my front porch surrounded by overgrown bishop's weed and a Power Rangers bike and a spider caught in a jar, and it's warm out and we're about to graduate from high school. And at this moment I feel like baby Emily, like nothing has gone wrong yet, like I have a whole new life in front of me.

MOST LIKELY TO SUCCEED

I'm a Most Likely. I made The List. They gave me an award. I know just because I'm on The List doesn't make me like Lindley, doesn't make me pretty or smart or talented. But it does make me singled out, special enough to be chosen by at least one person.

My dad got a Most Likely: Most Likely to Succeed. I wish I had known him then. I wonder what he was like, what about him screamed to others: This Guy's Going Somewhere. I'm not quite so glamorous: Most Likely to Write for *Teen* magazine. But it's okay; I'll take my recognition where it comes.

Especially if it's on the night of my senior banquet, on the sixth floor of a tower overlooking the whole Salt Lake Valley. If I could choose a place to have my name read out loud, it would be there, with all those students, my friends, the clink of china against crystal.

It was a beautiful night. All my friends, we looked so nice. The photographer said smile, and we did; it was that easy. Dancing was easy, too, last night. There was the boy I pretended to hate, the boy I pretended to love, the boy I pretended not to know, all asking me to dance with them, not caring that my feet couldn't move right and my Bad Hand was shaking and my arms were wet underneath.

And then it seemed like I really was Most Likely. To write for a magazine, to be the girl I had always dreamed of being, to succeed. There were those isolated moments of terror—the ones I'll always have—when I was afraid I was mocked, it was a joke, I was their entertainment, and not in a good way. I was this close to going back to being the sullen girl, the jaded girl, the backward girl.

But the paranoia passed. No time for it, because then I could see, as clear as if the words were painted on the ballroom floor in front of me:

Tonight, we are all the Most Likely to Succeed.

PAPA JOHN'S

My summer job starts when I hear that Utah's first Papa John's is opening, and it is opening down the street from me. Why anyone would want a state's flagship store in New Galilee I have no idea, but I'm not complaining.

We had Papa John's at Hollins. One night, the dining hall food was something burned and cold, and the salad bar had dwindled to dregs, and everybody was starving by eight fifteen. One of us got the idea to order pizza, and the closest place that delivered was Papa John's, and everybody had eaten Papa John's before except me. The pizza had a nice flavor and a chewy crust, and I liked how it came with little containers of dipping sauces. I mean, I didn't use them. But I like a good value.

It's always been the plan for me to have a full-time job this summer, the summer after I graduate from high

EMILY WING SMITH

school. It was the plan when I needed every ounce of money I could get to go to Hollins, and it's the plan now, because I'll still need money at BYU.

The job is delivered to my doorstep, like a gift from the pizza gods. The Monday before school gets out, I go to the near-completed Papa John's and interview for a job. Three days later, I'm hired. The next week, I start work as the assistant manager.

I'm given a dark green polo that fits like a muumuu and a Papa John's baseball cap. Wayne, our manager, is hard core about the hat. The one time I misplace it, he makes me go home, and I can't work until I find it.

A team comes in from PJ HQ down south to train us. Pizza is their world, and I note life lessons as I follow them around the store.

—Don't underestimate the value of cheese; treat the mozzarella like gold.
—Mushrooms are beautiful; watch that they don't turn ugly.
—Keep your eye on the pies while they're baking, and if you see a bubble form, pop it with the big stick. Taking care of the bubbles when they're small keeps them from becoming a big problem later.

Big Boss Bubba shows me how to slap dough. You start with a perfectly formed patty of yeasty, glutenous goodness, sprinkle Dustinator on the counter to keep it from sticking, and press your fingers about a half inch in, moving them around the dough.

When you do this, you're supposed to use both sets of fingers, but I quickly learn Bad Hand is not up to the task. I take it out of the equation and follow the rules for shaping and slapping dough, but follow them one-handed. It takes some trial and error, mostly error, but I've gotten a modified technique down. Big Boss Bubba puffs out her lower lip and shrugs.

I don't notice Wayne behind me until he says: "Huh. She's got a . . . unique way of doing that?"

Big Boss Bubba keeps her arms folded across her chest and says, "Hey, whatever works."

And again I think, *Yeah, whatever* does *work.*

ORIENTATION

"Hello, freshman class of Brigham Young University."

Funny how I never thought he'd be saying that to *me*. Funny how I swore I'd never again be a Popsicle stick, herded around with the masses. Funny how sure I was that I knew what I wanted.

"Today, I am standing before the most intelligent, best-prepared freshman class ever to enter BYU."

Funny how I'd snicker at that before, how even now I do on the outside. Funny how real all these feelings are that I never thought I'd have: feeling right here, feeling at home, feeling like I fit. Funny how unreal everything else feels: the large campus with its large buildings with their large lecture halls. The large feeling, my smallness and my part of the largeness, enveloping me in its enormity.

"You will face challenges and struggles during your

years here. You will work harder than you ever have before."

Funny how it was taking the French placement exam in the state-of-the-art language lab. How I sat down at the Mac and the mouse was already on the left-hand side, like it knew I was coming. Funny how everything I knew jumbled in my mind to find me in the position of ready to learn anything the university was ready to teach me.

"But you will have some of the most rewarding experiences of your entire life."

Funny how it felt registering for classes, then curling and uncurling the computer printout in my hand. *ENGL 310: Writing for Children and Adolescents. T/TH, 11:00 AM. Instructor: Plummer, Louise.* Funny how giddy I get from simply reading the words.

Funny how this was never what I pictured for myself, but now it's easy to imagine late nights with Kristin, with our other two roommates, all of us so close we're like best friends. Funny how we're all so different but somehow it works, like four distinct perfumes mingling pleasantly in sweet air. Funny how it's four of us in two rooms, but we're technically sleeping four in a row. Like it always should have been. Like it was at those sleepovers I never had.

"Welcome, freshman class, to the first year of the new millennium and your first year at this esteemed university. You have many things to look forward to."

Funny how much I believe him.

ON BEING BROKEN

After orientation there's a luncheon. The next four years of banquets flash before me: BYU-blue-rimmed china, the little plate on top of the bigger plate. Two goblets; a carafe of water and one with too-sweet red punch waiting to be spilled over the white tablecloth by a careless eighteen-year-old boy. I know what will come next: green salad from a bag, tomato wedge, three croutons. Ranch dressing in a gravy boat. Dry chicken, some kind of sauce. I bet dessert will be cake, and I bet an icing flower will be fluted on top, and I bet the icing flower will be BYU blue.

It is not what I wanted, but it feels like what I've secretly wanted all along. There is something pretend about a future I can't imagine. There is something real about imagining the banquets.

"Is this seat taken?" a fake-suave guy asks Kristin.

Black hair gelled back. Too-white teeth. An expression that, in a glance, runs across the rainbow of sincerity: wannabe friendly to friendly to smug. This is the kind of guy who wants to be known, the kind of guy who's starting small.

Kristin motions to the chair. He nods his appreciation, or maybe he's just agreeing with her decision, before he sits down. "I'm Jeremy." I expect him to hand me a campaign button or an order form, but he just leans in, taking up as much of the table as possible, and says: "This is my room-mate." Like a sidekick, or a backup singer.

"Bob," the roommate says. He smiles, maybe shy, maybe sick of his roommate.

I look at them both, and it's obvious who should be cuter. I've played this game since grade school, since Damien Topps, and now I'm an expert. Bob has curly hair and not-quite-right glasses, and his neck is longer than it should be. But he's so much easier to look at than Jeremy.

Jeremy grabs a roll and passes the bread basket to Kristin, not waiting for the blessing of the food which, knowing BYU, will start any minute. "I loved what the honors dean had to say, about how doing the honors pro-gram is like getting a Lexus after paying for a Toyota."

This guy is worse than I thought. I say what I'm thinking: "Really? I'd rather get a Toyota after paying for a Toyota."

They look at me: Kristin's early-stage eye roll, Bob's cocked head on his long neck, Jeremy's smirk. "Um, the Lexus is the much better car."

"I know." I shrug. "But I asked for a Toyota." A Lexus

isn't just a status symbol; it's a complication. My life has enough of those.

"You know it was just an example, right?" I can't tell whether Kristin is talking to me or to Jeremy. She passes the bread basket, and I take a roll but don't take a bite.

After the prayer, servers (BYU students in white shirts and blue bow ties) bring us salad. Three croutons. "So," Kristin says, picking off her tomato wedge, "where are you guys from?"

Jeremy mentions the town next to New Galilee, which surprises me zero percent. He and Kristin talk about the people they know in common. Her next-door neighbor was his soccer teammate. Of course.

"What about you?" I ask Bob.

"I'm from Virginia."

"Really?" Virginia. I'm hooked on Virginia. "What part?"

He shrugs, surprised at the follow-up. "Small town. Salem."

"By Roanoke?"

"Uh, yeah." He looks baffled, then pleased, then baffled. "You know Salem?"

"I've been there! I was taking a summer program at a college in Roanoke. Hollins? One night we went to a minor league baseball game in Salem."

"Did they win?" asks Kristin. Bob does not look optimistic.

"No. They lost by a lot. They aren't very good, are they?" I immediately realize I shouldn't say that, because aren't people insanely loyal to the home team? But Bob doesn't look offended. Just Jeremy does.

"Um, nobody in the minor leagues is very good." Jeremy's impatient for his turn to talk. "That's why it's called the *minor leagues.*"

I have a pretty strong desire to slap Jeremy. It's not a fleeting thought, either. I think: *Who at this table would be better off if I slapped Jeremy?* Then: *Right across the face so it won't do any lasting damage, but enough that he'll go away.* Thinking about it instead of doing it helps. I still want to slap him, but I won't. I don't *have* to. My body obeys my mind. Finally.

"Outside Salem, I have never met anybody who has been to Salem." Now Bob looks pleased, almost impressed, even. I don't know why it makes me pleased, too, but it does.

"Well, I'm not like anybody else," I admit.

"Yeah," Jeremy says. "We're getting that." In my mind, I see him rubbing his raw, stinging red cheek. "Pass the ranch."

I'm not like anybody else, and I don't care if Jeremy thinks that's a bad thing. Because seriously, who wants to be like Jeremy? I wouldn't necessarily say I like myself now, but I like myself a heck of a lot more than I like him.

So I say, "You know, I've been to doctors my whole life, lots of them, and none of them have been able to fix me."

Bob's salad fork pauses in midair, and he's holding it with his left hand, and he says: "Maybe you were never broken."

Dan. With him, I feel all better.

HOW IT HAPPENS

Meeting Dan is the magic bullet nothing else is. Not therapy or moving away from Kent or getting glasses. Not the accident that was supposed to save me, not getting the brain tumor removed and hoping the bad parts of me were finally cleared away. Not friends or writing or Most Likely or BYU or even God. Although when I think about it, it makes more sense than anything in my life ever has: God gave me Dan.

When I'm with Dan, I feel all better. The kind of better I don't even think to put into words at first, because I don't have to prove it (*hey, look, I'm better now, see?*). An organic, this-is-how-it-always-should-have-been better. Comfort without any compromise.

Something good happens to me where nothing good has ever happened to me before. Church. And not just church. Church volleyball.

On Thursday nights, all the college-age kids in town get together for Institute, a religion class. Most people stay after to play volleyball. I would not be staying after to play volleyball, but The Crew is here, so I do. It's summer, so we're finally reunited, and it's like we were never apart.

I sit on the edge of the gym stage and swing my legs, and I talk to whichever one of them rotates out until they rotate back in. So far I've got a conversation going with Lindley on the pros and cons of her new boyfriend, a conversation going with Kristin on the pros and cons of her zoology major, and a conversation going with Milla on the pros and cons of her current school, a university in Hawaii. "I think I need to transfer closer to home," she says, her eyes flicking between my face and a really tall girl I don't know, spiking the ball.

"Good," I say. "I've missed you on the mainland."

"Same." She gives me a side hug and jumps from the stage. "I'm up."

Since all three of them are playing now, I decide to watch, but it turns out I hate watching volleyball as much as I hate playing it, and as I'm figuring all this out, a guy comes up to me. He's wearing a white T-shirt with I ♥ MORMON GIRLS printed in red block letters, and I recognize him. Dan-no-last-name. My friends are always talking about him and pointing him out to me.

"Hey," he says. "You're not playing?" He doesn't say it all demanding, like I *should* be playing volleyball, and why aren't I? Not like other people have said to me about various activities all my life: *You're not playing Red Rover? Why on earth not? You're not doing the hokey-pokey? What's* wrong *with you?*

I'm glad Dan isn't a person like that. I don't put up with people like that anymore.

"I'm not good at volleyball," I tell him.

Dan nods.

"You know how some people say they're not good at volleyball, and then it turns out that while they're not *great* at volleyball, they're actually okay at volleyball?"

Dan nods.

"I am one hundred percent not one of those people."

Dan smiles, an easy, no-strings-attached smile that I get used to instantly.

"I'm Emily," I tell him.

"I know," he says. He leans against the stage with his arms back and pulls himself up next to me.

"What's up with your shirt?" I ask him. The red letters bleed a little, almost like he silk-screened it himself.

"I got it made in the Philippines," he says, "on my mission."

"Did you ever wear it?" Male Mormon missionaries wear white collared shirts and ties. They're only allowed to dress like regular people on P-Day, the day each week set aside for laundry and grocery shopping. I'm not sure wearing this T-shirt would ever make someone look like a regular person.

"Sometimes," he says.

"What did people think?" I had a Filipina pen pal, so I know most people there speak English, but would I ♥ MORMON GIRLS translate?

Dan shrugs. "I don't know what they thought." Again, his tone says so much. It's not defiant: *I don't know what they thought and I don't care!* His tone is so him, so *I never bothered thinking what people thought, because, you know, it doesn't matter.*

I like his answer.

"Hey," he asks, "do you have plans for tomorrow night?"

Tomorrow night's Friday, the weekend, so I'm sure The Crew will be doing something. I don't know what it will be, but I feel totally comfortable inviting Dan. Dan would love The Crew, and I already know they like him. It's exhilarating, having a group of friends and inviting someone new to join us. I'm like one of the Medallions. "My friends and I will be doing something. You can hang out with us!" I sound maybe a little too rah-rah, but whatever.

Dan looks at me a few seconds before he says anything. I've never noticed his eyes before: root-beer brown behind nice-guy glasses, ones that aren't showy or geeky. His face fits him perfectly. He says, "I was thinking it could be just you and me."

It maybe goes without saying that I don't date much.

Just you and me. *Just you and me.* In exactly two-thirds of a moment, his words go from taking me off guard to feeling completely natural.

Because in reality we've talked about volleyball and a

T-shirt. But already it feels like we've talked about everything, from Disneyland to chocolate milk to whatever's in between. Already I feel like I've always known Dan, and today I finally got to meet him.

With him, *just you and me* sounds exactly right.

EPILOGUE:

HOW I'M LIVING STILL

"Hey," says Dan, tapping lightly on my mostly open office door. Dusky light, the kind reserved for summer evenings, slants through my second-story window and illuminates him: thick black hair; strong, muscular body; and a smile that calms me every time I see it, even if I didn't know I was anxious. In all the best ways, he's completely different from Rembrandt. And he's real.

Dan comes over to my desk and rests his hands on my shoulders. They always get tensed up without my noticing when I'm at the keyboard for too long, typing in the modified, one-handed technique I've perfected over the years. I finally gave Bad Hand a break and stopped trying to touch-type, and now I *clickity-clack* at a respectable thirty-three WPM (only 11 percent below the average speed).

I end the quotation marks on my last sentence. Three

more chapters of my next YA novel—it's been a good day. "How was work?" I ask Dan, and swivel my chair around to face him.

"Good," he says. Dan's a computer programmer and doesn't give me details about it unless I press for them, since my computer skills fall into the just-learned-to-type-thirty-three-WPM category. "How's the writing?" He knows it's going well because it always is when I'm still in my office by the time he gets home, so all I do is nod. "You had an appointment with Iris today, too, right? How did that go?"

Iris is my health-care miracle worker. She knows all about my head injuries and complicated medical background, she gives me counseling *and* meds, she understands Woo-Head and Bad Hand better than anyone should have to. I'm not sure Iris knows how I'm living still, either.

"She says that she's proud of me." Even though I'm a grown-up now, I still get a weird satisfaction from pleasing other grown-ups. But pleasing Iris feels different, somehow. When Iris is proud of me, I know I'm getting all better, no matter what route I have to take to get there.

"That's great," Dan says. "Oh yeah, and what time is the signing tonight?"

Dang it. Why do I always do this? I get so lost in my writing I don't pay attention to the time. Most nights it doesn't matter, but tonight's important. It's the launch party for my friend Alexa's debut novel. Soon.

And I'm supposed to pick up Louise in ten minutes.

Yes, Louise. Louise Plummer. Last summer she and I were both invited to teach at a writing conference, and we were talking over lunch one day. I was eating my sandwich, and Bad Hand was shaky, and I was going to feel awkward, but then I didn't care anymore, because Louise was laughing at something, something *I* had said. And I listened to her laugh and wondered, *How is this my life?* Then she was talking about her neighborhood, and I realized it sounded a lot like my neighborhood, and that was when I discovered I live three blocks away from Louise Plummer.

So that's how I live now. Carpooling to writer events with Louise Plummer. Soon.

Luckily I've already painted my nails green, to match Alexa's cover. It's what everybody in our writers' group is doing to celebrate her book's birthday. But I still need to change into a better shirt, a clean one without a chocolate stain on the sleeve. "What shoes should I wear tonight?" I ask Dan in a panic, trying to save my document and finger-comb my hair at the same time.

"When are you going to stop asking me that? I *don't know.*" Dan rolls his eyes but is still smiling. "Wear whatever shoes you want." He pulls me out of my chair and kisses me. "You already look beautiful."

And it's funny, how much I believe him.

ACKNOWLEDGMENTS

I don't publicly thank God very often, but I Thank God for These People:

Thanks to the tireless Michael Bourret, who made this memoir happen, and to Julie Strauss-Gabel, who had a pretty big part in it, too. Thanks to everyone on the Dystel and Dutton/Penguin Young Readers Group teams, particularly Erin Young and Melissa Faulner.

My mom and dad taught me I was extra creative and extra left-handed and never for a second let me think that was a bad thing. It has made all the difference in my life. Juliana, thank you for growing up with me and becoming my best friend. To unnamed brother one (Ethan), unnamed brother two (Andy), and unnamed little sister (Hannah): Without you, there would be an unnamed, aching hole in my life.

Deepest gratitude to those who've joined my family and supported this memoir: Annie for reading early drafts; Shannon for being the wind beneath my wings; and Reo, Mike, Cami, Josiah, Ha, Andrea, Brian, Brent, and Yoriko.

The additions of Holden and Harper, Kelsey and Madison, Lincoln, Emma, and Kai make life so much sweeter.

I come from incredible stock. Gramma Wilson, you are an inspiration. Thank you for your wisdom, for your love, and for reading my blog. Thanks also to Grandma Wing, whose words "Emily Jane is who I want to be when I grow up" give me the strength to live a life worthy of them.

A special thank you to all my teachers in elementary school, junior high, and high school. I consider it an honor and a privilege that there are too many of you to thank individually.

Thank you to my therapists and doctors. You fought an uphill battle.

Everyone in Our Thing: Lauren Elkins, Vivian Evans, Megan Goates, Jennie La (Fortune), Emily Manwaring, Sarah Plummer, Amy Stewart, Julia Blue Wright, and Beck—words can't express what we have, so I'm not going to try. Luckily, I know you all know what I mean. Ann Cannon and Louise Plummer, thank you for bringing us together. The two of you are my life coach.

Perhaps the most fulfilling and unexpected part of my life as a writer is having the writing friends I do. The community at Glen West summer 2012 helped me as I began seriously drafting this book. The Swan Valley group helped me polish it. Rock Canyon is always there, the SIX has been the best friends a girl could have, and the Snowbunnies convinced me I had a story worth telling. Specifically, thanks to those who read this book in any of its many phases and offered feedback: Matt Kirby, Brodi Ashton, Kim Webb Reid, Francisco Stork, Sara Bolton, Anne Bowen, Ally Condie, Kristin Harmel, Kiki Sullivan, Alison Van Diepen, and Wendy Toliver.

I'm grateful beyond measure for the people who make my life so rich. You've all shaped this book in some way: Mindy and all the Kidds, Aymee Callister, Cammen, Nicole and Sara, and the women of Hollinsummer 1997. A shout out to my neighbors, my young women, my students, and Jersey Hanlon.

Thank you, God, because I'm living still.

Daniel, you make my story complete. You and me forever.

© MINDY KIDD

Emily Wing Smith is the author of *The Way He Lived* and *Back When You Were Easier to Love.* She is a graduate of Brigham Young University and received her MFA in Writing for Children and Young Adults from Vermont College of Fine Arts. Emily lives with her husband in Salt Lake City, Utah.

You can find her online at www.emilywingsmith.com.